Class and Status in America:
A Contemporary Perspective

By

John F. Sullivan

DORRANCE
PUBLISHING CO
EST. 1920
PITTSBURGH, PENNSYLVANIA 15238

Dorrance Publishing Co
585 Alpha Drive
Suite 103
Pittsburgh, PA 15238
Visit our website at *www.dorrancebookstore.com*

ISBN: 978-1-6376-4072-2
eISBN: 978-1-6376-4915-2

Class and Status in America:
A Contemporary Perspective

To Anne Sullivan, the wind beneath my wings.

TABLE OF CONTENTS

PREFACE

Today it is difficult to read a newspaper, watch television, or surf the internet for even a brief period of time without seeing "upper class," "social status," "working class," "income inequality," and related terms being used. Yet, these terms are never defined by members of the media even though they mean different things to different people. When Americans turn to academia for definitions and clarification they are met by "word blizzards" of ill-defined terms and concepts. Consider the following excerpt from Wikipedia's current (2020) discussion of social class:

> "… a set of concepts in the social sciences and political theory centered on models of social stratification which occurs in class society, in which people are grouped into a set of hierarchical social categories, the most common being the upper, middle, and lower classes … However, there is no consensus on a definition of 'class' and the term has a wide range of sometimes conflicting meanings."

What is needed are well-defined terms and concepts that explain how an individual's socioeconomic class is determined in contemporary America as well as how Americans in different socioeconomic classes live. The principal purpose of this book is to propose those terms and concepts, to describe the Country's current class structure, to describe the lives of lower-class, middle-class, and upper-class Americans, and to consider a number of changes that have been proposed to the current class structure.

In Chapter 1 the evolution of socioeconomic classes in America is described. In Chapter 2 the two economic criteria (income and wealth) used to determine the socioeconomic class of today's Americans are defined and discussed. Poverty is also discussed in this chapter. Chapter 3 presents, for purposes of discussion, a nine-level class structure for contemporary America. Chapter 4 consists of a description of the lives of lower-class Americans. Chapters 5, 6, and 7 describe three concerning trends in the Country's current class structure — growing inter-class economic differences, economic segregation, and reduced inter-class mobility.

Chapter 8 contains an explanation of how the two economic criteria (income and wealth) discussed in Chapter 2 combine with each American's social status to determine his or her socioeconomic class. The four sets of criteria used to determine one's social status are also introduced in this chapter. They are: family background, personal achievements, appearance, and behavior. The proposed conceptual model is shown in the box on the top of the next page.

Each of the criteria used to determine an individual's social status are discussed in greater detail in Chapters 9 through 13.

> Economic Criteria = Income + Wealth
>
> Social Status = Family Background + Personal Achievements + Appearance + Behavior
>
> Socioeconomic Class = Economic Criteria + Social Status

Chapter 14, "Class Detective" contains a series of three exercises. Each of the exercises begins with a description of an American adult in a contemporary setting. The reader is then asked to use the six criteria and sets of criteria in the proposed conceptual model to estimate the person's socioeconomic class and to speculate on his or her past and future.

Chapter 15, consists of a summary of the information and concepts presented in Chapters 1 through 14, as well as the writer's suggestions for addressing three major problems with the Country's current socioeconomic class structure. The three problems are income/economic inequality, economic segregation, and a low level of inter-class mobility.

There are a number of statements and assertions made throughout this book. When appropriate and possible these are supported by research data and references to other sources. When such data and references are not provided, these statements and assertions are, in the writer's judgment [a] common knowledge or [b] simply the writer's opinion based on his own observations and research.

Nothing in this book is intended to state or imply that members of the upper class are uniformly better, smarter, or more hard-working than other Americans. That is simply not

John F. Sullivan

the case. It is doubtful that anyone in this country works harder and is under more pressure than a lower-class family trying to raise children.

CHAPTER 1:
BACKGROUND

There probably has never been a society where everyone is treated equally. Inevitably some people live better, are more respected, and have more wealth and power than others. There are different strata or classes in every society. This was certainly true in seventeenth century Europe where the upper class consisted of the titled nobility and the "landed gentry." The titled nobility and the landed gentry typically owned large country estates as well as small towns and villages that they inherited from their ancestors. They administered their estates and were financially independent, living off of the rents and crops produced by their properties. At that time in Europe there was little, if any, interclass mobility. The rich were very rich, the poor were very poor, and if you were born poor, you were going to die poor.

The extreme wealth and life-style differences between the upper and lower classes as well as the near-impossibility of members of the lower classes moving up were two of the principal reasons so many Europeans came to America. They were seeking a society with less extreme differences between the lives of the upper and lower classes as well as a society where deserving members of the lower-class could move up, get ahead. That was the American Dream. It is no coincidence that the United States Declaration of Independence states that "All men are created equal."

Socioeconomic Class in Early America

In the early settlements and colonies on the East Coast of America most people were farmers and shopkeepers and there were only moderate differences in income, wealth, and life styles. The American dream was alive, hard work paid off, and there were minimal barriers to inter-class mobility. But as time went on, economic development permitted an increased division of labor, additional occupations were created and occupational differences in income emerged. In addition, some farms and shops grew faster than others, corporations were formed, and some corporations did better than others.

Soon, family differences in income, wealth and life styles began to widen in cities such as Boston, Philadelphia, and New York. Many of the Nation's most prominent universities were established in those cities and that's where American art and culture first garnered world-wide attention and acclaim. In Boston, members of the emergent upper-class were referred to as "Boston Brahmins," a term coined by physician and writer Oliver Wendell Holmes in 1860. "Brahmin" refers to the highest ranking caste of people in the traditional caste system in India.

Boston Brahmins were wealthy merchants, land-owners and employers. They were politically conservative and almost all were members of Unitarian and Episcopal churches. They espoused high moral and ethical standards, were reserved in appearance and behavior, were patrons of the arts, and were active in civic affairs. Many of them became prominent in academia as well as local, regional, and national politics. Boston Brahmins and their families were widely respected and admired. The Lowell and

Cabot families were two of the best-known Boston families and may have been America's first "elites." A famous toast from that period is shown below.

"And this is good old Boston,

The home of the bean and the cod,

Where the Lowells talk only to the Cabots,

And the Cabots talk only to God."

In New York City during the 1880s Louis Keller, a newspaper columnist began publishing the Social Register which was a directory of upper-upper class American families. Wikipedia describes the families chosen for inclusion as "Well-connected, "patrician" families from the Northeast United States"; "White, Anglo-Saxon Protestant (WASP) families from the East Coast;" and members of "polite society." A more cynical article in the Chicago Tribune in 1985 stated that aspiring registrants needed "plenty of green (money), blue (blood), and (to be) lily white."

In addition to listing the names and addresses of its registrants, the Social Register listed their club memberships and "academic affiliations." The publication described itself as "The only reliable and trusted arbiter of society in America." It gradually lost credibility and influence during the 20th century, was purchased by Malcom Forbes in 1975, and is now owned by Christopher Wolfe.

Contemporary America

It is clear from the brief history described immediately above that money, race, ethnicity, and religion played significant roles (explicitly or not) in the determination of one's socioeconomic class in the Country's early days. This, despite the founders' declaration that all men were created equal.

Things began to change in the middle of the 20th century. Cultural norms and standards were challenged then as never before. In the 1960s and 1970s there were nationwide protests against the Vietnam War and for civil rights; against social injustice and pressures to conform and for greater personal freedom. Bras and draft cards were burned. In 1964 the Civil Rights Act was passed and it became illegal to discriminate on the basis of race, ethnicity (national origin), and religion in everyday business and financial decisions. After that it was no longer acceptable or legal to treat or differentiate among Americans based on race, sex, ethnicity, and religion.

During the last three decades of the 20th century and into the early years of the 21st century the protests against social injustice and pressures to conform and for greater personal freedom continued in various forms e.g., "Occupy Wall Street," "Black Lives Matter," and "ESG investing."

In the middle-to-late 20th century, it also became clear that the East Coast was no longer dominant in terms of wealth creation, the arts, education and culture. Dramatic wealth creation was occurring on the high-tech West Coast — dynastic wealth that would propel the Gates (Microsoft) and Bezos (Amazon) family fortunes beyond those of the Morgans and the Rockefellers. West Coast colleges and universities such as Stanford, The University of California at Berkley, and the California Institute of Technology became rivals of the most prestigious East Coast colleges and universities.

It should be noted that the creators and executives of today's high-tech West Coast firms do not have their roots in East Coast Brahmin and WASP families. The current CEOs at Microsoft and Google were born in India and are neither white nor Anglo-Saxon. It is also unlikely that they are politically conservative. Both are reportedly free-trade advocates, pro-immigration (not open immigration) and human-rights advocates

The racial, ethnic, religious and political criteria used to assign Americans to socioeconomic classes in prior years can no longer be used for such a purpose, at least not explicitly so. This does not mean, however, that America has become a classless society where everyone is equal. There is indeed a class structure in 21st century America. The criteria used to determine socioeconomic class, however, are different than they used to be. Income and wealth remain very important; family background, ethnicity, religion, and political conservatism are probably less so; personal achievements probably more so, behavior probably far more so, and one's appearance, how he or she looks, continues to count.

CHAPTER 2:

THE ECONOMIC CRITERIA

The two economic or financial criteria most often used to describe the socioeconomic class of Americans are household income and household net assets (wealth).

Household Income

The household income data cited most frequently are collected and reported by the U.S. Bureau of the Census. The Census Bureau household-income data include the annual income of every member of each household over the age of fifteen. This includes pre-tax wages and salaries, pre-tax investment income, and income from governmental assistance programs such as unemployment insurance, workers' compensation, and Social Security. It does not include employer-paid premiums for insurance and retirement income programs.

In 2019 the median aggregate annual American household income was $68,703. This means that the aggregate annual income of about half of American households was above $68,703 and half were below $68,703.

Only 5% of households had aggregate annual incomes above $270,002 and only 10% had incomes below $16,026. As shown in the table below there was significant variation in household income by race and type of household.

ANNUAL AGGREGATE HOUSEHOLD INCOME, 2019

Type of Household	All Households Percent of Median	Income
Race		
Asian	5%	$98,174
White Non Hispanic	66	76,057
Hispanic	14	56,113
Black	13	45,438
Family Households	65	88,149
Married Couples	49	102,308
Female HouseholderWith No Spouse Present	12	48,098
Male Householder With No Spouse Present	4	69,244
Nonfamily Households	35	41,232

Source: Current Population Surveys, U. S. Bureau of the Census.

Among racial groups, black and Hispanic households had the lowest 2019 aggregate annual income. Because income and wealth remain important determinates of socioeconomic class in America it is logical to infer that blacks and Hispanics will be over-represented in the Country's Lower Class and that, in fact, is the case.

The type of household with the highest 2019 median income according to the Census Bureau was the Married Couple household ($102,308). A big part of the explanation for this type of household's having such a high income level probably has to do with both spouses' working.

Poverty

The Census Bureau defines poverty as regularly or frequently experiencing deprivation with respect to the basic necessities of life such as food, clothing, shelter, and health care. Each year the Census Bureau publishes "Poverty Thresholds" which are annual income levels below which households are considered to be living in poverty i.e., poor. Poverty thresholds are published by the number of people in the household. For example the Bureau's 2019 poverty income thresholds for three-person and four-person households were $20,335 and $26,172 respectively. During 2019 the Bureau reported that about 11% of American households or approximately 36 million people were living in poverty. Other researchers have estimated that another 14% (those in households with incomes between $26,000 and $50,000) were living in "near poverty" or on the verge of poverty in 2019.

The key take-away statistic with respect to poverty is that approximately 25% of Americans or slightly over 80 million people, those with annual household incomes of $50,000 or less, are living in or on the verge of poverty. Black and Hispanic households as well as non-family households are far more likely to be in poverty than are other households.

The Bureau does not provide poverty income thresholds based on the cost-of-living in different American states or cities but there is no doubt that there are substantial cost-of living differences among them. A family of four with a 2019 annual income of $26,000 might be poor in Waco, Texas but it would be desperately poor if not homeless in New York City.

Household Wealth

The wealth data used most often to analyze socioeconomic class in the United States are collected and reported every three years by the Federal Reserve Bank. Household wealth can be thought of as the aggregate assets (e.g., a home, automobile, money in saving accounts, and investments) of the members of a household minus any of their outstanding liabilities (e.g., mortgages, credit card debt, and student loans.)

The 2016 Federal Reserve Survey of Consumer Finances (SCF) data indicate that the **top one percent** of American households had median net assets of $10,300,000 or more, **the top five percent** of households had median net assets of $2,400,000 or more, fifty percent had household net assets of $97,000 or less, and the bottom ten percent of households had a **negative** net worth of a least $1,000.

There were significant racial differences in the wealth and the types of assets owned by American households in 2016. As shown in the table below, white households had median net assets (wealth) of $171,000 compared with $17,600 for back households and $20,7000 for Hispanic households. The most frequently owned asset by American households was a vehicle of some kind — a truck or a car. There were significant racial differences in home ownership, ownership of retirement accounts, and ownership of publicly-traded stocks. There are many reasons for these differences but the biggest reason may be that it takes discretionary income to build wealth and, as shown above, the incomes of white households are much higher than the incomes of black and Hispanic households. Being willing to make investments in such things as retirement accounts and publicly-traded stocks and bonds is also critical.

NET ASSETS (WEALTH) BY TYPE OF HOUSEHOLD, 2016

Head of Household	White	Black	Hispanic	Other
Median Net Assets	$171,000	$17,600	$20,700	$64,800
Type of Asset Owned (% of Households)				
Primary residence	73%	45%	46%	54%
Vehicle	90	73	80	80
Retirement Accounts	60	34	30	48
Family-owned business equity	15	7	6	13
Publicly-traded stocks	61	31	28	47

Source: Survey of Consumer Finances, Federal Reserve Bank. 2016.

The same Federal Reserve survey found that approximately 40% of all Americans reported that they either wouldn't be able to cover an unexpected $400 expense using their savings or credit cards and that they would have to borrow money or sell something to do so. This percentage has been relatively stable for many years and may well go up in post-Coronavirus America.

CHAPTER 3:

A PROPOSED CONCEPTUAL MODEL

The writer suggests that a three-by-three matrix be used to conceptualize, describe, and analyze America's current socioeconomic class structure:

PROPOSED THREE-BY-THREE STRUCTURE

Lower Class	Middle Class	Upper Class
Upper lower class	Upper middle class	Upper upper class
Middle lower class	Middle middle class	Middle upper class
Lower lower class	Lower middle class	Lower upper class

Dividing any country's population into different socioeconomic classes is an inherently arbitrary and subjective process. There are always two questions that must be answered. The first is: "How many levels or classes should be used?". And the second is "What criteria should be used to define the levels".

How Many Levels (Classes)?

The right number of levels (classes) exists when there is general agreement that [a] there is little or no difference in the socioeconomic class of people assigned to the same level (intra-class homogeneity) and [b] the socioeconomic class of the people at any one level is discernibly higher than that of the people in the level below it (inter-class heterogeneity).

Three classes e.g., "Lower class," "Middle Class," and Upper Class" are not enough to use to describe America's current class structure. Doing so would result in putting people whose socioeconomic classes are clearly different into the same class thus violating the intra-class homogeneity rule.

Anything higher than a nine-level structure, on the other hand, would probably violate the inter-class heterogeneity rule and force people whose socioeconomic classes are essentially the same into different levels. The writer, therefore, proposes the three-by- three structure shown above for purposes of analysis and discussion.

Economic Thresholds and Levels

It is further proposed that the initial assignment of individuals to the nine-class structure be based on their household incomes and wealth and that their social statuses be used to modify the initial assignments, up or down, as appropriate.

Upper-Class Economic Thresholds (Top 5%)

The three-tiered upper class in the proposed nine-class socioeconomic class structure is limited to individuals in households with incomes and net assets (wealth) that are in the **top five percent** of all American households. Therefore, and based on the Census Bureau and Federal Reserve Bank data discussed in the previous chapter, someone would need to be a member of a household with an aggregate annual income of at least $270,000 and net assets of at least $2,400,000 to be considered upper class. It is around these levels of income and wealth that the distinctive features of upper-class lives become possible. These include impressive homes, second homes, private schools, private clubs, jewelry, expensive clothing, servants, luxury travel, and investments. It is acknowledged that the proposed upper-class income and wealth thresholds are actually higher in high cost-of-living areas such as New York, San Francisco, Alaska. and Hawaii.

The very top tier top of the upper class, the **upper-upper class,** is limited to those households whose incomes and wealth are in the **top one percent** of all American households. Based on Census Bureau and Federal Reserve Bank data this means that only individuals in households with aggregate annual incomes of about $400,000 or more and net assets of $10,000,000 or more will be eligible for inclusion in the upper-upper class. These are "the one-percenters," 'the elites," and the "millionaires and billionaires" often referenced in the media.

Of the two economic criteria, income and wealth, the latter (wealth) may be more important. Incomes can change dramatically from year to year. Net assets tend to be more stable and to grow over time. It is better, more-secure, therefore, to have an upper-upper class life style supported by a high level of net assets as opposed to a high income. The most economically secure of the upper class are financially independent. They seldom worry about money. Moving up the socioeconomic ladder for them has usually been a matter of turning high incomes into income-producing assets and/or inheriting substantial financial assets.

It is possible to establish socioeconomic classes above the proposed upper-upper class based on even higher levels of income and wealth. The top one-tenth of one percent of American households had median net assets of more than $43,000,000 in 2016. These households, however, represent such a small portion of all households that it is not worth establishing additional socioeconomic classes to accommodate them. In addition, there is a point, perhaps above $10,000,000, where additional wealth does not result in an appreciable difference in one's financial security or life style.

Given that the annual income and net asset thresholds (minimums) for the lower upper class are $270,000 and $2,400,000 respectively and $400,000 and $10,000,000 for the upper-upper class, and based on a process of liner interpolation, the proposed income and wealth thresholds for the middle-upper class are $335,000 and $6,200,000 respectively. (See table below.)

PROPOSED ECONOMIC THRESHOLDS
BY SOCIOECONOMIC CLASS

Class (% Of All Households)	Proposed 2020 Thresholds (Minimums)	
	Annual Income	Net Assets (Wealth)
Upper- Class (5%)		
Upper- Upper (<1%)	$400,000	$10,000,000
Middle- Upper	335,000	6,200,000
Lower-Upper	270,000	2,400,000
Middle-Class (70%)		
Upper-Middle	< 270,000	< 2,400,000
Middle-Middle	160,000	250,000
Lower-Middle	50,000	1,000
Lower-Class (25%)		
Upper-Lower	< 50,00	Zero
Middle- Lower	38,000	Negative
Lower-Lower	< 26,000	Negative

Lower-Class Economic Thresholds

At the other end of the proposed nine-class conceptual model is the Lower Class. The three-tired Lower Class includes all members of households with aggregate annual incomes of $50,000 or less and negative household assets. As noted previously, this will include a total of approximately 25% of Americans (nearly 80 million people) who are living in poverty (in households with aggregate annual incomes of less than $26,000) or on the verge of poverty (households with aggregate annual incomes of $26,000 to $50,000.

Middle Class Economic Thresholds

The economic thresholds for the three-tiered Middle Class begin where the economic thresholds for the three-tiered Lower Class end. Since the thresholds for the Lower Class end at <$50,000 (income) and zero (wealth), the proposed economic thresholds for the Lower Middle Class are $50,000 (income) and $1,000 (wealth). The economic thresholds for the three-tiered Middle-Class end where the thresholds for the Upper-Class begin. Since the thresholds for the Upper Class begin at $270,000 (annual income) and $2,400,000 (wealth) the proposed thresholds for the Middle Class are < $270,000 (income) and <$2,400,000 (wealth).

With these thresholds in place, the income threshold for the Middle-Middle Class can be determined through a process of liner interpolation and it is $160,000 The wealth threshold for the Middle-Middle Class if determined in the same way would be $1,200,000 but based on Federal Reserve Survey data this figure is too high. Thus, the wealth threshold for the Middle-Middle class is arbitrarily set at $250,000.

With an aggregate annual household income of $50,000 or more, a middle-class life-style becomes possible i.e., the basic necessities of life are taken care of; the members of the household can afford a home and/or a car; and some money is available for the education of children, retirement, and/or investments. Once again, it is acknowledged that the economic thresholds proposed herein for the middle class would need to be higher for high cost-of-living areas such as New York, San Francisco, Alaska, and Hawaii.

Since, in the proposed conceptual model, twenty-five percent (25%) of the Country's households fall into the three-tiered lower class and five percent (5%) fall into the three-tier upper class, the remaining seventy percent of households fall into the three-tiered Middle Class The proposed economic thresholds for all nine so-cioeconomic class are shown in the above table.

A Nine-Story Condominium

One way to think about the Country's current socioeconomic structure is to think of it as a nine-story condominium building. Each floor has its own entrance or elevator and is noticeably nicer than the floor below it. The families on the top three floors are different from the families on the bottom three floors and they hardly know each other. Their children go to different schools, they eat at different restaurants, and they have different health-care providers. There is some, but not much, floor-to-floor movement in the building. People born on one of the nine floors are likely to live on that floor all their lives,

Most people in the building prefer to spend time with others living on the same floor as they do or on the floor immediately above or immediately below theirs. They are most comfortable with the people on those two floors; they can "be themselves" around them. They have a great deal in common. They come from similar backgrounds and have similar interests, values, and tastes.

The same cannot be said for the people living two or more floors above them. Although most of those people are unfailingly courteous and polite, they are harder to get to know; are more distant. They seem to come from different backgrounds and have different interests. and values. They even dress a little differently.

In general, residents are not inclined to spend much time with people living two or more floors below them either. The people living on those floors appear to be good, hard-working Americans but people with whom they don't have much in common. Some of them come from different racial and ethnic backgrounds. They seldom see them outside the building,

CHAPTER 4:

THE LOWER CLASS

The Lower Class, approximately 25% of all Americans, is composed of two groups of people. The first, and by far the largest, group consists of those who are in the Lower Class solely for economic/ financial reasons. Their aggregate annual household incomes are below $50,000 and they have little, if anything in the way of net financial assets. Some of these people may be trusted, respected, and held in high regard by other Americans. Their social status doesn't matter. They are poor or nearly so and therefore members of the lower class. For purposes of discussion this first group will be referred to as **low-income or low-paid** Americans.

The second group assigned to the three-tiered Lower Class are Americans whose incomes and wealth qualify them for membership in the middle-class or even the upper-class but who are held in low regard by other Americans. These are **low-status** as opposed to low-income Americans. Their low status may be attributable to their occupations e.g., clearly criminal occupations such as drug dealers, sex traffickers, and organized crime figures. Or, it may be due to behavior on their part that is not criminal but clearly predatory and exploitive e.g., slum landlords, physicians who over-prescribe opioids or other drugs for profit, predatory lenders, and dishonest business people. Alternatively it may be due to behaviors that other Americans find objectionable —

bad manners or bad habits such as excessive drinking or the constant use of profanity. Finally it may simply have something to do with the way they look or dress. For whatever reason, the social status of these Americans is low. Other Americans do not want to be around them or be associated with them. They are consigned to the Lower Class despite their incomes and wealth.

The Lives of Lower-Income/Paid Americans

As discussed in Chapter 2, the median aggregate annual incomes of black and Hispanic households are well below those of white households. It is inevitable, therefore, that based on income and wealth alone, blacks and Hispanics will be over-represented in the Lower Class. As the Bureau of Labor Statistics data in the table on the top of the next page show, there is a strong positive correlation between education and income in America which means that Americans with a high-school education or less will also be over-represented in the Lower Class.

Further, employees with hourly-paid jobs will be over-represented in the Lower-Class simply because they are generally (there are always exceptions) paid less than salaried employees. Most hourly-paid jobs are "manual" jobs that require their incumbents to work with their hands. Manual jobs are sometimes referred to as "blue-collar" jobs and include unskilled (e.g., farm workers, laborers, material handlers, and janitors), semi-skilled (e.g., painters and delivery drivers), and skilled jobs (e.g., electricians and plumbers). The occupants of hourly-paid, white-collar service, administrative support, and technical jobs also fall into the Lower

**EDUCATION, ANNUAL EARNINGS,
AND UNEMPLOYMENT, 2019**

Education Level	Median Annual Income	Unemployment Rate
Less than high school	$12,314	5.4%
High school	38,792	3.7
Bachelor's degree	64,896	2.2
Master's degree	77,844	2.0

Note: 2019 Bureau of Labor Statistics data
for full-time wage and salary workers, not households.

Class. Examples of these jobs include maids, housekeepers, servers, cashiers, clerks, secretaries, and technicians of various kinds.

Many low-income jobs are temporary, part-time, and "gig" jobs which offer little in the way of job security or employer-paid benefits such as health-care insurance, retirement income, and paid-time-off. Because of the low pay as well as the fact that these jobs are temporary, part-time, and gig jobs, low-income/paid Americans often work two or more jobs, some of which may be "off the books." Off-the-books jobs are those in which incumbents have no employer-paid benefits and are paid in cash.

Low-paid jobs are often with contractors to the Nation's largest employers. A contractor's employees may clean the offices at Apple's headquarters but they will not be not invited to Apple's Holiday party nor will they have the job security and employer-provided benefits that Apple's employees have.

Stress and Job Satisfaction

Low-paid jobs may also be more stressful and less-satisfying than they once were. Because of technological improvements such as closed circuit television, constant communication devices, and blockchain technology, the performance of people on these jobs is closely monitored whether the work is performed on a factory floor, in a delivery truck, or at home.

A Pew Research Center survey in 2016 found a negative correlation between income and job satisfaction. As shown in the table below only 39% of Americans with jobs that pay less than $30,000 a year were satisfied with their jobs whereas 59% of Americans with jobs that paid more than $75,000 were satisfied with theirs. This is not surprising and it's probably not just the money. As discussed above, many low-income/paid jobs in the United States today are stressful and offer little in the way of job security or employer-paid benefits.

JOB SATISFACTION AND HOUSEHOLD INCOME

Household Income	Very Satisfied
>$75,000	59%
74,999 to 30,000	45
< 30,000	39

Source: Pew Research Center Survey, 2016.

The unemployment data shown previously indicate that lower-income/paid Americans have an elevated probability of being unemployed. Other data indicate that they have lower life expectancies. A Harvard University analysis of 1.4 billion Internal Revenue Service records by Chetty et. al. (2016) found a high positive correlation between household income and life span. American men from the wealthiest households were found to live, on the average, fifteen years longer than American men in the poorest households. The difference in life span between the wealthiest and poorest American women was approximately ten years.

Life expectancy has been increasing in the world's advanced economies for decades if not centuries. The U.S. Center for Disease Control (CDC), for instance, reports that the average life expectancy for someone born in the United States in 1900 was 47.3 years compared with 78.9 years for someone born in the United States in 2020 (81.4 for women and 76.3 for men). The 2020 average life expectancies in the United States, however, is five or so years lower than the average live expectancies found in other advanced economies. This is largely because U.S. mortality rates plateaued in 1970s while the rates in other countries have continued to decline.

In a recent book entitiled *Deaths of Despair and The Future of Capitalism* the authors assert that a surge in deaths among white middle-aged Americans due to suicide, alcoholism, and drug overdoses is the major reason for the plateauing of mortality rates in America. These three types of "deaths of despair" rose from 31 per 100,000 in 1990 to 92 per 100,000 in 2017. The authors attribute the rise in deaths of despair to diminishing prospects for working/lower income Americans and the fact that their incomes have failed to keep up with inflation since the 1970s:

"In America money buys access to better healthcare, and beyond that, life is easier when you do not have to worry about how you are going to pay for a car repair, or childcare, or an unexpectedly large heating bill. Financial worry can suck the joy out of life and bring on stress which is often a trigger for pain and ill health."

The authors of *Deaths of Despair* further assert that the diminishing prospects and stagnant incomes of working/lower class Americans are largely attributable to globalization and technology-based productivity improvements. In this assertion they are in agreement with nearly every other social scientist and economist interested in the country's socioeconomic class structure. These two forces (globalization and technology-based productivity improvements, notably robots) are universally acknowledged to have reduced the demand for unskilled and semi-skilled employees, weakened the unions that once represented so many of them, and caused their incomes to stagnate.

Increasing rates of deaths of despair has been especially notable in Appalachia. This is at least partially attributable to a decline in the coal-mining industry. Coal mining brought high-paying jobs and relative prosperity to Appalachia in the early twentieth century. Since then, however, the country has been moving away from coal as its primary energy source. The number of coal miners has come down from a peak of 850,000 in 1923 to about 50,000 today. This has plunged hundreds of thousands of Appalachian families into the Lower Class and many into poverty. In 2016 J. D. Vance wrote a compelling autobiography describing his growing up in Appalachia. In his book, *Hillbilly Elegy*, he wrote:

"It is in greater Appalachia where the fortunes of working

class whites seem dimmest. From low social mobility, to poverty, to divorce and drug addiction, my home is a hub of misery."

Marriage and Divorce

It should be noted that low income/paid Americans are less likely to be married and more likely to be cohabiting and/or divorced than are their Middle-Class and Upper-Class counterparts (See table below). The 2020 overall marriage rate in the United States is around 50% which is down from approximately 65% in 1970. The sharpest drop has been in the lower class. Low-income Americans with part-time, temporary, and gig jobs; no health insurance; and no hope of ever retiring comfortably are not good marriage prospects and they know it. Others know it too. Thus, low-income/paid members of the lower class are less likely to get married or to stay married. In doing so they miss out on the economic and emotional benefits that marriage can bring.

PERCENT OF AMERICAN ADULTS
MARRIED, COHABITING & DIVORCED

Class	Married	Cohabitating	Divorced
Poor	26%	39%	46%
Working Class	39	10	41
Middle & Upper Class	46	5	30

Source: 2015 Census Bureau data as reported in "The Marriage Divide," Institute for Family Studies, 2017.

Data shown are for American Adults ages 18 to 55. "Poor" includes those with household incomes below the 20th percentile, "Middle & Upper Class includes those from households above the 50th percentile.

It was not always this way in America. Before the 1970s the vast majority of Americans got married and stayed married and most children lived in stable, married-couple households. Sometime in the 1960s, however, things began to change. First, poor Americans became markedly less likely to get and stay married. In the 1970s and 1980s working-class Americans followed and sharp inter-class differences in marriage and divorce rates emerged.

Retirement

Many low income Americans are going to have a difficult time retiring. In the United States, the federal government provides retirement income benefits as a part of its Social Security program. The federal government always intended that its Social Security benefits would supplement employer-provided retirement income benefits as well as income from retirees' savings and investments.

In the 1970s an assembly-line worker at an automotive company who had pre-retirement annual earnings of $24,000 and 30 years of service might retire with an annual retirement income of $20,000 which included an employer-provided pension benefit of $13,000, a Social Security benefit of $6,000 and $1,000 a year from personal savings and investments. At that time, a retiree from an automotive company would also be covered by employer-provided health insurance during his retirement years.

All of this provided for a secure and dignified retirement comparable to the retirement benefits provided assembly-line workers in other advanced economies. But things have changed since the 1970s. Due to rapidly-accelerating costs, and the need to compete in international markets, America's private-sector employers have been attempting to reduce their retiree income and benefits expenditures. Many have replaced defined-benefit programs with defined-contribution (e.g., 401k and 403b) programs and most have eliminated or reduced their retiree health benefit programs.

Unlike defined-benefit retirement income plans (pensions), defined-contribution plans are voluntary i.e., employees may chose not to participate. If they do chose to participate, employee contributions are required. Employers neither guarantee nor are responsible for investments or the level of benefits provided by defined-contribution plans (They were responsible for both with defined-benefit programs.) The low paid employee, therefore, is much more on his or her own and subject to the vicissitudes of the securities markets when he or she participates in a defined-contribution retirement income program.

At the same time that the switch to defined-contribution plans was occurring in the private sector, the Federal Government has been attempting to reduce its costs for "entitlement" programs including Medicare (health insurance for people over 65) and Social Security. In addition, and as has been noted previously, the net assets (wealth) of lower/working class Americans is negligible and in many cases, nonexistent. Thus, the three-legged stool (pensions, savings and Social Security) that was counted on to provide a secure and dignified retirement for the working class in the last decades of the 20th century has disappeared. Their wages have stagnated making it difficult to save, pension plans in the private sector have all but disappeared and Social Security is under attack.

The data in the table on the next page show the participation of Americans ages thirty-two to sixty-one in employer-sponsored defined-benefit and defined-contribution retirement plans in 2016. The first thing to note with respect to the data in the table is that only about 63% (19% + 44%) of working Americans participate in any type of employer-sponsored retirement income plan. The other 37% will need to rely entirely on Social Security and any savings they have been able to accumulate prior to retiring.

The second thing to note in the table is that more than twice as many working Americans participate in defined-contribution (e.g., 401k and 403b) plans as opposed to defined-benefit (e.g., pension) plans. It is likely that the defined-benefit plans that continue to exist are overwhelmingly in the public sector.

Finally, it should be noted that in the largely private-sector, defined-contribution plans, where participation is voluntary, the participation rates for lower income employees are far below the participation rates for higher-income employees. As stated above, low-income/paid employees live paycheck to paycheck and worry about money all the time. Most of them find it impossible to set aside money for retirement. Even when they do participate in defined-contribution plans it is at levels far below those necessary to provide meaningful retirement income benefits.

**RETIREMENT INCOME PLAN
PARTICIPATION RATES, 2016**

Employer-Sponsored Plans	Defined-Benefit Plans	Defined-Contribution Plans
All Americans Age 32 to 61	19%	44%
Household Income		
Bottom Quintile (20%)	6	10
Second Quintile	14	33
Middle Quintile	19	48
Fourth Quintile	32	62
Top Quintile	25	70
Race		
White Non-Hispanic	21	51
Hispanic	13	28
Black	17	33

Source: Federal Reserve Survey of Consumer Finances, 2016.

A recent (2019) nationwide survey conducted by the Pew Research Center among currently employed adults found that about one in four (42%) doubted that they would be able to collect **anything** from Social Security when they retire and another 42% thought that they would receive some Social Security retirement income but at lower levels than the benefits currently being provided. Consistent with these views, a large majority of survey participants were of the opinion that most Americans would need to work into their seventies in order to be able to afford to retire. The fact, however, is that unless something changes, unless some of these trends are reversed, the majority of low-income/paid Americans are never going to be able to afford to retire.

Stressful, low-paid, part-time, temporary and gig jobs with no or minimal job security and employee benefits; constant worries about money, shorter life spans, higher probabilities of deaths of despair; lower probabilities of successful marriages; and ever-diminishing hopes for comfortable retirements — that's what lower paid/income Americans (a quarter of the Nation's population) are facing. As discussed in the next chapter, this has not always been the case in this country.

Post Covid-19

The current (2020) pandemic may hasten changes in the lives and prospects of low income/paid Americans. Many health-care workers on the front line battling the virus are life-long members of the Lower-Class. They include ambulance drivers, food-service workers, nurse aides, and custodians. In addition, there are others who are not on the front line but who must continue to work during the pandemic. They can't afford to stay home. Many of these people provide much-needed services e.g., warehouse workers, postal workers, police officers, delivery drivers, and cashiers. Both of these groups of low income/paid Americans will have risked their lives every day during the pandemic. Inevitably they will have higher infection and death rates during the pandemic than members of the Middle-Class and Upper-Class. This is because [a] they are poor or nearly so and, therefore, have less access to health care than other Americans and [b] they could not or chose not to stay home during the pandemic. The public is increasingly aware and appreciative of these members of the Lower Class. It is hard to imagine that the low pay, minimal employer-provided benefits, stress and insecurity associated with their jobs will be allowed to continue post-Covid.

It should also be noted that the stock market, which declined precipitously at the outset of the pandemic, regained its equilibrium after a few months and went on to new highs. Very, very few low income/paid Americans have significant investments in the stock market. The exceptional post-Covid gains in the market, therefore, will redound almost entirely to the benefit of the middle-class and upper-class thus widening the wealth gap between the rich and poor in America.

CHAPTER 5:

ECONOMIC GROWTH AND INEQUALITY

The lives and prospects for lower-income Americans were not always as bleak as they seem in 2020. The best years for these people, and arguably for all Americans, may well have been from 1945 to 1975. Because of a seven-fold expansion in the Nation's gross domestic product (GDP) during this thirty-year period, economists sometimes refer to it as "the Great Expansion" or "the Golden Age of Capitalism". It could also be called the "Golden Age of the Working Class".

America's Golden Age

In 1945, what Tom Brokaw termed "the greatest generation" of Americans won World War II (WWII) and brought freedom to hundreds of millions of people in Europe and Asia. Members of the Country's armed forces were heroes around the world. America itself was looked up to as never before. If anything, the Nation's reputation was enhanced by its behavior **after** 1945. At that time, instead of occupying and confiscating wealth and property in Germany and Japan, America spent billions of dollars rebuilding and bringing democracy to those nations. A few years later America stopped the expansion of a communist dictatorship into

South Korea and brought democracy and prosperity to that country too.

During this period (1945 to 1975) America, in concert with its WWII allies and other nations of the world, created a number of multi-national organizations with the intent of fostering international trade and resolving international disputes peacefully rather than through armed conflict. Most prominent of these organizations were the United Nations, NATO, the World Trade Organization and the World Health Organization. America's leadership role in the creation of these organizations was very much appreciated by other countries and America became the most respected as well as the most powerful nation in the world.

During this same thirty-year period America made great progress on the civil/human rights front at home. Americans of all races, religions, ethnicities, and socioeconomic classes had fought together shoulder-to shoulder in WWII and the Korean War. They got to know each other as human beings. They realized how much they had in common and they earned each other's respect. Segregation based on race, religion, or ethnicity became less tolerable. The Country's armed forces were integrated shortly after the end of WWII and the Civil Rights Act was passed in 1964. The Civil Rights Act made it illegal to discriminate based on race, religion, or ethnicity in housing, employment and virtually all other transactions. Other laws were passed in the 1960s and 1970s prohibiting discrimination based on age, gender, sexual orientation, and disability.

All of these statutes improved the employment, income, and

inter-class mobility prospects for lower-class Americans particularly black and Hispanic Americans.

The Country expressed its appreciation to WWII veterans in a number of tangible ways.

It significantly expanded the Veterans Health Administration (VHA) which provides free life-time medical care to veterans, it established the VA home loan program in 1944 providing government-backed mortgages to eligible veterans, and, in the same year, it passed the GI Bill of Rights which provided four years of higher-education funding for eligible veterans. These three programs, like the civil rights statutes cited above, also had positive effects on the employment, income and inter-class mobility prospects of veterans.

As stated above, there was a seven-fold expansion in the economy of the United States from 1945 through 1975. The Country's Gross National Product (GDP) increased from $228 billion to just under $1.7 trillion. In 1975 the Nation's GDP represented some 35% of the world's economy and was three times larger than that of Japan, the next largest economy. There were some shallow recessions along the way but it was a period of nearly full employment in which the growth in the economy was widely shared by lower, middle, and upper-income Americans. Incomes roughly doubled during this period and this was equally true for lower, middle, and upper-class Americans. Inter-class disparities in income growth had not yet emerged.

The post-WWII world wanted what America was producing — refrigerators, automobiles, airplanes and computers; and it wanted these things in quantity. American companies grew and their profit margins were high. "Made in America" was stamped on thousands of products shipped overseas and it meant something. No other country had the ability to produce such high volumes of high-quality products.

Hourly-paid jobs with U.S. manufacturing companies, most of which required a high-school education or less, came with health insurance and pension benefits. There was a high demand for labor and large percentages of hourly-paid employees were represented by labor unions. Children followed their parents into blue-collar manufacturing jobs expecting to spend their entire careers with the same employer as their parents had.

The incomes provided by these jobs were often high enough to allow an hourly-paid employee to get married, buy a house and a car, take his or her family on vacation, and think about sending his or her children to college.

The exhilarating and halcyon days of "The Great Expansion" came to an end in the last few decades of the twentieth century By that time America no longer had the world's markets for manufactured goods all to itself. Employers in other countries began producing refrigerators and automobiles and later, airplanes and high-technology products. Profit margins for American manufacturers began to shrink and cost-cutting became imperative, not just to sustain profit margins but to survive in an increasingly-competitive world-wide economy. In order to reduce labor costs American manufacturers opened offices and plants in low-wage countries and contracted with suppliers in those countries. This phenomenon came to be know as "globalization."

American manufacturers also attempted to reduce their labor

costs by replacing hourly-paid employees with high-technology/automated equipment e.g., welding machines and computer-operated assembly and painting equipment — robots or simply "bots." These cost-reduction and productivity-improvement efforts on the part of manufacturing and even nonmanufacturing employers led to a reduction in demand for unskilled and semi-skilled jobs in the United States. This in turn, reduced the bargaining power of unskilled and semi-skilled Americans as well as the unions representing them.

Disparities In Income Growth

Beginning in the 1970s the incomes of lower income/class and middle income/class Americans began to grow more slowly than the incomes of the upper class. A 2020 report from the Pew Research Center, for example, cited the Census Bureau data shown in the table shown immediately below.

MEDIAN INCOMES:
AMERICAN HOUSEHOLDS, 1970-2018

Household	1970	2000	2018	1970-2018 Increase
Lower-Income	$20,000	$28,200	$28,700	43%
Middle-Income	58,100	81,700	86,600	49
Upper-Income	126,100	192,200	207,400	64
Upper As % of Lower	630%	681%	722%	

Source: Pew Research Center analysis of
Census Bureau/BLS Current Population Survey

As will be noted, the difference between the median incomes of lower-income and upper-income households went from 630% in 1970 to 722% in 2018. The Pew Research Center's income thresholds used to define lower, middle, and upper income households are slightly different than those chosen by the writer in Chapter 3 but the key point remains — the incomes of lower-income and middle-income families in America have been growing considerably more slowly than the incomes of upper-income families ever since the mid-1970s. This fact is corroborated by other Census Bureau data which show that, from 1967 to 2017 the incomes for the bottom ten percent of American households grew by abut 35% whereas the incomes for the top one percent grew by approximately 85%.

Perhaps more importantly, the "real" (adjusted for inflation) incomes of lower-income and middle-income families have been declining ever since the mid-1970s. From 1970 through 2018 the cost of living in the United States increased by approximately 55%. The incomes of lower-income and middle-income households, which increased by 43% and 46% respectively during the same period, therefore not only failed to keep up with increases in the incomes of upper-class households, they also failed to keep up with increases in inflation.

The data in the above table do not reveal the most stunning income-growth during this period i.e., the income growth for the highest-income households. These data are available in a second 2020 Pew report. In that report Pew researchers estimate that the average annual income of the **top 5%** of American households grew by approximately 100% from 1979 to 2017 while the average annual income for the **top 1%** grew by 157% during the same period. Both of these growth rates dwarf the 64% reported by Pew for the all upper-income households from 1970 to 2018.

Gini Coefficients

"Gini Coefficients" are commonly used to measure a nation's level of income equality These coefficients can range between zero (perfect equality) to 1.0 (perfect inequality).

According to the Organization for Economic Cooperation and Development (OECD) the 2017 Gini Coefficients for the most economically developed (i.e., the G7) nations range from a high of 0.434 for the United States to a low of 0.326 for France. Thus, income inequality in America as measured by Gini Coefficients is now higher than that found in any other large advanced economy.

As shown above, the growing inter-class disparity in income in the United States since the 1970s is not a matter of the lower-class doing nicely and upper-class doing much better. It is more a matter of lower-class and middle-class income growing slowly while upper-class income grows faster and, in the case of the upper-upper class, much faster. This inter-class income disparity in America has grown from a gap to a chasm. It is now larger than the interclass income differences found in other advanced economies and is viewed as inequitable by many Americans.

The reasons for the relative decline in the incomes of low income/paid Americans are complex but, as discussed above, among the most important are globalization and technology-based productivity improvements.

It may get worse. A December 2018 Pew Research Center survey found that 73% of the Americans participating in the survey expected the incomes of lower-income Americans to continue to grow more slowly than those of other Americans through 2050 and 69% of the survey participants stated that this was likely to be "a bad thing" or "a very bad thing" for the Country.

The Growing Wealth Gap

Inter-class differences in wealth are also increasing in America. The data shown in the table below are from the Federal Reserve Bank survey discussed in Chapter 2. These data show that the median wealth (net assets) of the top one percent of households increased by 28% from 2013 to 2016 — from $8,100,000 to $10,300,000. This increase in wealth was nearly three times as large as the increase in wealth for the typical (median) American household over the same period ($83,900 to $97,000 thousand)

MEDIAN INCREASES IN
HOUSEHOLD WEALTH 2013-2016

Household Wealth	2013	2016	Increase
Top 1%	$8,100,000	$10,300,000	28%
Top 5%	1,000,000	2,400,000	23
Median	83,900	97,200	10

Part of the reason for the inter-class disparity in the recent growth in household wealth has to do with the nature of the assets owned by different households. The principal asset of most households is the homes themselves (See table in Chapter 2.) Retirement income assets and publically-traded stocks are two other major asset categories for Americans. As noted previously, lower-income/class Americans have very little in the way of retirement savings. With respect to publicly-traded stock, a recent (2020) Gallup survey found that stock ownership is highly-correlated with household income and that 84% of heads of households with incomes of $100,000 a year or more owned stocks whereas only 22% of the heads of households with incomes of less than $40,000 owned stocks.

Since 1970 (SP 500) stock prices have been increasing more than twice as fast as home prices. Thus, one of the reasons the rich have gotten richer in America and the inter-class wealth gap has widened in the last fifty years or so is the disproportionate ownership of retirement savings and stocks by higher-income households.

"It takes money to make money."

CHAPTER 6:

ECONOMIC SEGREGATION

There has been some level of economic segregation in this country since the mid-1800s e.g., box versus bleacher seats at professional baseball games, first-class versus coach seats on planes, several levels of accommodations on cruise ships, and poor versus wealthy neighborhoods. The extent of economic segregation, however, has been increasing ever since the 1970s — about the time that inter-class differences in income and wealth began to increase. The lives of the rich and the poor in America are increasingly different and separate.

Housing

Census Bureau housing data show that since 1970 more Americans live in uniformly affluent neighborhoods and uniformly poor neighborhoods as opposed to mixed or middle-income neighborhoods. In 2014 Bischoff and Reardon reported:

> "In 1970, 65% of families lived in middle-income neighborhoods; by 2009 only 42% did. The proportion of families living in affluent areas almost doubled from 1970 to 2009 as did the proportion of families in poorer areas."

Increased economic segregation in housing was facilitated by the building of the inter-state highway system, the expansion of suburbs, and the movement of many middle-income and upper-income families to the suburbs during the "Great Expansion" (1945 - 1975). Initially there was not a high level of economic segregation in the suburbs. Most suburban homes were modest and unpretentious (e.g., Levittown, NY). Later, however, as greater differences in income and wealth emerged, some suburbs and homes became far more expensive and impressive than others.

Today, gated communities in the suburbs anchor the high end of the American housing spectrum. Wikipedia estimated that there were 20,000 or so gated communities in America in 2020. While this number (20,000) may be more or less accurate, there is no doubt that gated communities are far more prevalent than they were in the 1950s and 1960s particularly in affluent parts of the country.

There is a wide variety of gated communities but they are virtually all [a] residential i.e., composed of homes rather than mixtures of homes, offices, and commercial enterprises and [b] developed for middle-income and high-income families, not the poor. These communities limit access to their neighborhoods by using fencing, walls, and gates of some sort in order to limit access to home owners, service people and guests. Some gated communities are far more serious about limiting access to their communities than are others. Some, for instance, are fenced but have only an unattended gate house to discourage outsiders from entering. Others have 24/7 security forces and community-wide surveillance/alarm systems. Gated communities all have some form of common or shared amenities. These might include parks, walking trails, swimming pools, tennis courts and/or a club house. Gated communities also have homeowners associations (HOAs) or property owners associations (POAs) which maintain the common areas and amenities.

The principal attractions of gated communities to the upper-middle-class and the upper class are privacy, security, and prestige.

The most prestigious and expensive gated communities are characterized by:

- Spacious houses and/or condominiums set well back from roads and streets.

- A variety of architectural styles for free-standing homes.

- An absence of vehicles on streets and driveways (They are in home-owners' garages).

- 24/7 security forces and community-wide surveillance/alarm systems often monitored by private-sector security services

- Secure and well-maintained perimeter walls/fencing.

- Tastefully-designed and well-maintained amenities, common areas, and landscaping.

In major metropolitan areas such as New York, Miami, Chicago and San Francisco prestigious co-op and condominium buildings function in much the same way as gated communities in the suburbs. That is, they attract upper-middle-income and upper-income residents by offering spacious, well-maintained units as well as superior levels of privacy, security, and prestige. Such buildings have 24/7 doormen or security personnel in order to control access to the buildings. The most common amenities provided are indoor parking, fitness centers, and swimming pools. These buildings have homeowners' associations that perform the same functions as the HOAs and POAs in gated communities.

The principal criticism of gated communities and, to a lesser extent, prestigious co-ops and condominiums is that they have adverse effects on social cohesion. That is, the residents of such communities and buildings seldom send their children to local public schools or rely as heavily on public services as do members of the broader community. Thus, they are less willing than their neighbors to support, financially and otherwise, local schools, police forces, fire departments, and other public service agencies.

For example, the members of a gated community may be willing to pay $500 a month to their HOA to maintain the security of their homes but unwilling to vote for a tax increase to support a city-wide police force. Or, a condominium owner in a prestigious building with two children in a private school may be willing to contribute to that school's endowment but unwilling to vote "Yes" on a tax increase intended to improve city-wide or state-wide schools.

At the low end of the housing spectrum are manufactured homes, commonly referred to as "mobile homes" or "house trailers." Initially these were manufactured in a factory on a wheeled chassis and towed behind a car or truck. They became popular in the 1950s and 1960s at the time that America's highways and freeways were being modernized. They were used by families for vacation travel and for temporary housing on construction sites and elsewhere. They were relatively small at the time — eight feet wide and under 400 square feet.

Beginning in the 1970s, however, the mobile home industry bifurcated. House trailers were replaced by recreational vehicles and manufactured homes. A recreational vehicle (RV) is a housing unit built on a truck chassis. RVs can be driven like a truck rather than being towed behind another vehicle. They are used in the same way that people used mobile homes originally. That is, for vacation travel and temporary housing on construction sites and elsewhere.

The manufactured housing industry, on the other hand, produces housing units intended for long-term or permanent installation elsewhere often on a masonry foundation. These housing units are not produced on a chassis, cannot be towed behind a car, and must by moved by a professional trucking company. Manufactured homes are larger than the original mobile homes and are now marketed as inexpensive permanent housing.

According to Manufactured Housing Institute (MHI), approximately 90,000 manufactured homes ranging from 400 to 900 square feet will be built and sold in this country in 2020 at an average cost of $80,000. The overwhelming majority will be installed in "mobile home communities" (the term "trailer park" is no longer used.) According to the MHI the number of manufactured homes produced in the United states each year has increased by 49% since 2015.

According to the most recent Census Bureau estimates, approximately 22,000,000 Americans live in manufactured homes and their annual household incomes are a little **less than half** of the median American household income — $30,000 as opposed to $60,000. Thus, it is definitely lower income/paid Americans who live in manufactured housing. Many of them rent as opposed to own their manufactured homes.

Because of the relatively low level of inter-class mobility in America, anyone who owns or lives in a site-built home of 2,500 square feet or more has probably never been in a manufactured/mobile home. Conversely, if someone is living full-time in a manufactured home, the chances are good that he or she has never lived in a site-built home of 2,500 square feet or more.

Professional Sports Venues

There have been modest levels of economic segregation among people attending professional sporting events in America for many years e.g., box versus bleacher seats at professional baseball games. But today the level of economic segregation at professional sports events has reached levels that could not possibly have been imagined by earlier generations of Americans.

In a recent (2020) book entitled: *The Velvet Rope Economy: How Inequality Became Big Business* Nelson Schwartz discusses ticket prices at Yankee Stadium. The first thing that should be mentioned is that there are no fixed prices for tickets to individual home games. Instead, the prices vary game-by-game depending on demand right up to the day the game is played. The overall average price for a single ticket in the "nose-bleed" far upper deck is around $40. All the other tickets are more expensive and there is a wide variety to chose from. At the top of the pyramid, however, are the "Legends" seats. These are seats in the first few rows of the lower deck between home plate and third base and between home plate and first base. The single-game prices for these seats are said to vary between $500 and $1,000. There is a private entrance for fans with Legend-seat tickets as well as other premium-seat tickets. Further, there are private, up-scale restaurants available for each level of premium seating.

This level of economic segregation in professional sports was unheard of until the 1960s. It may have begun with the opening of the Houston Astrodome in 1965 which is about the same time that major inter-class differences in the growth of income and wealth began to emerge. The Astrodome was the first stadium to offer glassed-in, climate-controlled skyboxes. Now private suites, separate entrances, and exclusive high-end restaurants can be found in all professional sports venues.

Perhaps the most startling contemporary example of economic segregation in professional sports can be found in the Chase Arena. This is the home of the Golden State Warriors of the National Basketball Association in San Francisco. Season ticket holders in the new arena must secure their right to purchase season tickets every year by first purchasing a "Personal Seating License" (PSL) and only then purchasing tickets. According to Schwartz the cost for a PSL for a four-seat "mini suite" (not a glassed-in, climate-controlled private suite) in 2020 started at $350,000 and the games tickets, which were several hundred dollars each were additional. PSLs are now common in professional sports venues. Commenting on this phenomenon, Schwartz wrote:

> "Just going to a game has shifted from being a blue-collar pursuit to a white-collar one a couple of generations ago. Now even well-off professional and midlevel executives find themselves priced out with only the top one tenth of one percent left in the desirable seats."

College Sports

It didn't take major colleges and universities long to adopt the economic-segregation strategies now common in professional sports. These strategies include premium parking, exclusive and catered "tail-gate" parties, private entrances, exclusive high-end food service, and glass-enclosed, climate-controlled suites — all for a price. PSLs are still relatively rare in college sports and they take a different form there. For instance, some universities require membership in a "Varsity Club," "Alumni Club," "Supporters Club," or something similar in order to purchase season tickets. Tickets are then made available to club members depending on how much they contribute to the club or university each year.

A high level of economic segregation in the distribution of tickets to college and university sports events was uncommon in the 1960s and 1970s. In those days students and alumni were given preference when purchasing tickets and loyalty counted too. If you were an alumnus and had purchased season tickets for twenty years in a row, you would not have ended up in the end zone for a football game or in nose-bleed seats for a basketball game. Now, if someone else is willing to pay more than you are for season tickets, you might.

It is easy to understand extreme levels of economic segregation in professional sports.

There, it is unabashedly all about the money. But in college sports, where all of the institutions are not-for-profit, why does money always seem to trump institutional affiliation and loyalty? To be fair, money doesn't always overwhelm all other considerations particularly in the case of smaller colleges and universities as well as those that have chosen to deemphasize intercollegiate sports. When it comes to attendance at football and basketball games at major ("big-time") colleges and universities, however, not everyone is afforded the same experience and money talks.

Prestigious Colleges and Universities

As discussed previously, Americans who graduate from colleges and universities are likely to have higher incomes than those who do not. Further, those who graduate from prestigious colleges and universities (those with low acceptance rates) do even better.

In a recent (2019) book entitled *The Years That Matter Most: How College Makes or Breaks Us*, author Paul Tough cites research showing that students who attend prestigious colleges and universities have about a one in five chance of ending up in the top 20% of income earners, students attending community colleges have about a one in 300 chance, and people who don't attend college at all have about a one in 1,000 chance.

Over the past fifty years or so, as the link between a college degree and future earning has became stronger and more well-known, two thing have happened. First, the most selective American colleges and universities have been deluged with applications including many from outside the country. And second, the cost of a college education has risen more than three times as fast as households incomes in America. This has resulted in the cost of a college education at a four-year college or university being out of reach for many middle-income and lower-income families. Paul Tough cites research showing that more than two-thirds of the undergraduates at the most prestigious colleges and universities come from families with incomes in the top 20% of the national income distribution whereas only about 4% come from families in the bottom 20% of the income distribution. This will be discussed in greater detail in Chapter 10.

The fact that a college education for their children, particularly at a prestigious institution, is unaffordable is a particularly hurtful form of economic segregation for middle-class and lower-class families. It's one thing to accept the fact that you are never going to graduate from college and another thing to accept the fact that your children have no chance of doing so either.

VIP Health Care

Concierge physicians are primary care physicians, usually internists or family practice physicians, who receive annual fees (salaries) from their patients. These fees are out-of-pocket and not reimbursed by public or private-sector insurance. The start at about $1,500 per-patient, per-year and go up from there. The fees are not regulated by insurance firms or government agencies. In exchange for such fees, concierge physicians agree to maintain reduced patient loads (e.g., 300 versus the 3,000 or so for other primary care physicians) and to provide higher levels of service to their patients. These services might include 24/7 telephone access, same-day appointments, no or minimal waiting times, home visits, help in scheduling visits with specialists, and help in dealing with the health-care system in general. For instance, if a patient of a concierge physician were having chest pains the patient might call the physician and the physician might tell him to go to the emergency room at a local hospital immediately. If the patient did so he might well find his concierge physician there waiting for him and the emergency-room staff well-prepared for his arrival.

Concierge physicians were relatively rare in the United States until the late 1990s but Wikipedia now estimates that there are 1,000 to 5,000 of them. They serve upper-middle-income and upper-income patients, not the poor. This form of economic segregation is relatively new but growing in America.

Also growing are VIP (very important person) floors or wings in hospitals and medical centers. Rooms and suites in these units are available for out-of-pocket fees that are neither reimbursed nor regulated by insurance companies or government agencies.

There is very little information available about VIP floors or wings but the information that is available indicates that the fees start at $750 or so per-patient, per night. VIP rooms and suites are, of course, private and they are generally more spacious and well-appointed than other patient rooms. They may, for instance, contain interesting art work, wide-screen televisions with premium channels, wi-fi, and luxury bedding. Further, they are likely to have better views and be more secluded and quieter than other rooms. If they are suites, the second room adjoins the patient's room and can be used as a sitting room or an extra bedroom for the patient's family members, a private-duty nurse, or a servant of some kind. Premium, on-demand food service is also standard.

A review of the healthcare literature reveals that many healthcare practitioners, notably nurses and physicians, are not comfortable with the increasing prevalence of concierge physicians as well as VIP rooms and suites i.e., "VIP Healthcare." It offends some of their senses of social justice. Healthcare executives, on the other hand, view VIP Medicine as an economic necessity. They know that some hospitals and medical centers would simply go out of business if they had to depend solely on Medicare and Medicaid reimbursement levels.

Economic segregation in healthcare, like economic segregation in higher education, is particularly hurtful for lower-income Americans particularly the thirty million or so with no healthcare insurance. It is difficult to accept the fact that a serious illness may drive your family into bankruptcy or that you and members of your family may be forced to accept third-rate healthcare or be denied healthcare altogether.

Shopping

In the 1950s and during the last decades of the 20th century, shopping centers and later shopping malls, were built at a furious rate across America. Some were enclosed and most were "anchored" by large department stores where middle America liked to visit and shop. Prominent among these anchor stores were Sears, J.C. Penney, and Macys. A few up-scale malls and shopping centers anchored by higher-end retailers such as Nordstroms and Saks Fifth Avenue were also developed and so were a number of lower-end , discount or "outlet" malls. It was a bell-shaped distribution with the largest number of shopping centers and malls serving middle-income Americans.

As income inequality grew, middle-income malls and shopping centers began to disappear and their middle-income anchor tenants began to fall into financial difficulty. Middle-income and lower-income families switched their alligence to newcomers such as Walmart, Costco, and dollar stores.

Up-scale malls had better survival rates although they started to lose business to on-line retailers, notably Amazon. It's not that upper-income families never shop at Walmart or Costco. They do, but for groceries and household products not for apparel, footwear, or jewelry For middle-income and lower-income families, however, Walmart and Costco are one-stop shopping centers and that includes shopping for apparel, footwear, and jewelry as well as groceries and household products. Up-scale grocery stores and chains e.g., Whole Foods came along about the the same time as Walmart and Costco and began to attract upper-income families from old-line middle-class grocery chains such as Kroger and

A&P. The net effect of all of these changes is that rich and poor Americans don't shop at the same places as much as they used to.

Lexus Lanes

Other forms of economic segregation that have developed recently include the "Lexus Lanes" discussed in the Schwartz book referenced previously. Lexus Lanes can be found on over forty freeways and expressways in busy metropolitan areas. Most Americans are familiar with High Occupancy Vehicle (HOV) lanes on freeways and expressways. These (HOV lanes) are the typically the innermost two lanes of four or six lane freeways and expressways. The lanes were originally intended to encourage car pooling and reduce traffic congestion. Thus, they were initially restricted to vehicles with at least one passenger in addition to a driver. Because of this restriction these lanes were not crowded and traffic moved much faster that it did in non-HOV lanes.

Some metropolitan areas now allow access to HOV lanes to one-passenger cars, for a price. Their ability to do so came about with the advent of the EZ pass technology now common on toll roads across the Country. With this technology drivers affix a transponders to their windshields and high speed cameras record the presence of their vehicles on toll roads and in HOV lanes. States or municipalities then use the transponder data to collect fees from accounts previously established with the agencies by the owners of the transponders. These accounts are typically established by check or credit card. The problem is that many lower-income/paid Americans have neither a credit card nor a checking account. They are, therefore, unable to us EZ Pass toll roads or Lexus Lanes on freeways and expressways. Even those that have credit cards or checking accounts would probably be less willing to pay tolls than higher-income Americans. Lexus Lanes are an example of cash-strapped government agencies imposing a new form of economic segregation on lower income/class Americans There were no Lexus Lanes on the nation's freeways and expressways in the 1950s when they were built.

Television Watching

Television watching became an option for Americans shortly after the end of World War II i.e., in the mid-to-late 1940s. TV sets showed up in the homes of the upper class at first but gradually became ubiquitous in American households. From the early days of television through the 1970s television watching was free in the United States. Once a family purchased a television set, it could watch television day and night at no additional charge. In the early days there were a limited number of things to watch on television and families from all socioeconomic levels watched the same programs. Those were the days of broadcast television where nearly all of the programming was provided by three broadcast networks — ABC, CBS, and NBC. The cost of this programming was paid by advertising. Companies paid the networks to run commercials for their products.

In the late 1970s Cable Television came along. Cable companies offered TV "bundles" that included the major networks plus a number of additional channels such as CNN, ESPN, the Food

Channel, and The Home and Garden Channel. Cable TV bundles, however, were not and are not free. Even though the programming offered by cable companies still contained commercial advertising, American consumers began paying monthly fees to the cable companies. In 2020, these fees generally range between $100 and $200 a month depending on the channels and services selected by consumers.

In the early 2000s internet-based "streaming services" became another option for television viewers. These services are available in addition to or "over the top" of the programming provided by cable companies. The two most popular streaming services are Netflix and Amazon Prime. The charges for streaming services are in addition to cable TV charges and are generally in the range of $10 to $25 a month. The one significant advantage of streaming service programming is that it is **commercial free.**

The number of advertising minutes per hour of programming on the major networks as well as cable TV channels is now (2020) approximately eighteen minutes per hour. It was approximately nine minutes per hour in the 1960s. In the European Union it is currently limited to twelve minutes per hour.

Eighteen minutes per hour is just too much for many Americans. A recent (2019) survey by Deloitte found that most Americans were comfortable with up to eight minutes of commercials per hour of programming but that sixteen minutes was "too much" and that twenty minutes was "was way too much." Too many commercials as well as the high cost of cable TV has produced what is now know as "cord cutting" in American. Millions of middle-class and upper-class Americans are dropping their cable TV services and searching for better (cheaper and more commercial free) ways to watch television.

Many lower-income/class Americans simply cannot afford cable TV or streaming services. If they can, they can afford "basic cable" where there are limited viewing options and viewers are bludgeoned by commercials on a nightly basis

The Digital Divide

Laptop computers and the Internet emerged on the scene in the United States in the late 1990s. In combination they are probably the most important communication and learning tools ever invented. The internet is a electronic network that can be used to connect virtually any two computers anywhere in the world. It is indeed an electronic "worldwide web" for computers and other devices. With a computer, a cell phone, or certain other electronic devises someone can send an **"email"** (written message) to someone else anywhere in the world and have it (the message) arrive almost immediately.

The internet can also be used to search for information from all kinds of sources around the world. If a high-school student, for instance, wanted to learn something about Canadian history he or she could use the internet to search for relevant information in thousands of libraries as well as other research centers around the world. Using the internet today's students can take for-credit courses offered "on-line" from hundreds of colleges and universities. Someone interested in Canadian history could probably sign up for and take an on-line, for-credit course in the subject at the University of Toronto. To use an over-used adjective, the internet is truly amazing. Motivated individuals can use it to inform and educate themselves to an extent never before possible.

Computers and access to the internet, however, are not often free. Computers and printers must be purchased and access to the internet requires the purchase of supporting hardware as well as the service of an Internet Service Provider (ISP). Thus, not every American household has access to a computer or the internet. As the data in the table below show, only about half of American households with aggregate incomes below $30,000 have access to computers and the internet whereas 94% of households with aggregate annual income of $100,000 or more do. This difference in access is often referred to as the "digital divide." It is a crucial divide. It helps keep poor Americans uninformed and poor.

COMPUTER AND INTERNET ACCESS: 2019

Household Income	Percent of Households That Own A Computer	Percent of Households That Have Internet Access
Less Than $30,000	54%	56%
$30,000 to $99,999	83	81
$100,000 or more	94	94

Data Source: Pew Research Center Survey, May, 2019

Criminal Justice

In 2018 Professor Sandra Trapper of Penn State University summarized seventy years of surveys of U.S. prison populations by stating, "This research leaves little doubt that most of the people serving time for criminal offenses in the United States come from the lower end of society's socioeconomic continuum. They are more likely to be unemployed, be less educated, and earn less than the general population."

There is an on-going debate about how much of the over-representation of the lower class in the Nation's prisons can be attributed to their committing more crimes and how much can be attributed to their being treated more harshly by the criminal justice system than members of the middle class and the upper class. Those who argue that the poor are treated more harshly and unfairly allege that it is attributable to the facts that the wealthy can afford better attorneys and that they have better connections, better educational backgrounds and better employment histories than their lower-class counterparts.

Another way in which that the poor are treated more harshly than the rich in the criminal justice system has to do with bail. Posting bail, usually in cash, allows those charged with a crime to remain free while awaiting trial. The wealthy are far more likely to be able to do so than the poor who are, therefore, much more likely to spend pre-trial time in jail. Pretrial diversion is another example of how the poor are treated more harshly than the rich by the criminal justice system. Pretrial diversion programs allow the wealthy to avoid trials altogether, for a price. The price usually entails their signing up for some sort of educational program e.g., an anger management or traffic safety program and agreeing to some sort of court supervision program for a period of time. Participation in pretrial programs can be quite expensive and most of the programs are run by for-profit corporations under the auspices of court systems.

In the Schwartz book referenced previously, the author describes another way in which the wealthy can be treated less harshly than the poor by the Country's current criminal justice system — "pay-to-stay jails." The example he describes is the City of Santa Ana, California. The city's jail has a number of private cells which convicts can rent for $110 a night rather than stay in the county jail which is considerably less pleasant and more dangerous. It's is hard to imagine economic segregation being more obvious and onerous than it is in the Santa Ana jail.

Another concern of civil rights organizations is the increasing enforcement of criminal laws against the homeless for things like loitering and sleeping in public places. Civil rights agencies see these enforcement activities and the fines associated with them as exploiting and harassing the poor and a violation of basic human rights. Those claims, however, fall on the deaf ears of cash-strapped court systems and criminal justice agencies.

CHAPTER 7:
INTER-CLASS ECONOMIC MOBILITY

Economic inequality and economic segregation in a society are more tolerable if they are not extreme and if there is a high level of economic mobility. Economic mobility — the opportunity to move up financially from working class to middle class to upper class — is the "American Dream." That's why so many people immigrated to America and why so many still want to do so. And they don't want economic mobility only for themselves. They want it at least as much for their children.

While economic opportunity and mobility may be the dream for Americans the fact is that those goals are more easily stated than achieved. According to a 2012 Pew economic mobility analysis 43% of children raised in the bottom quintile (bottom 20%) of the American income distribution remain in the bottom quintile as adults and 40% of children raised in the top quintile remain there as adults. Most movement up or down in the socioeconomic class structure in America are relatively modest e.g., from lower-middle-class to middle middle-class. Multi-level moves in the structure are rare. Only about 8% of Americans raised in the highest income quintile (top 20%) drop to the lowest quintile (lowest 20%) as adults and only about 4% go the other way — from the bottom to the top quintile.

In 2020 the World Economic Form (WEF) an independent research organization headquartered in Geneva produced a report ranking socioeconomic mobility in eighty-two countries. The WEF analysis was not based on outcome measures such as income or wealth. Instead, it was inferential. That is, the researchers selected five societal characteristics that they thought promoted socioeconomic mobility and then ranked the eight-two countries on those characteristics. The characteristics were: accessibility to high-quality health care; accessibility to high-quality and life-long education; accessibility to information technology (computers; the internet, and etc.); job opportunities and employment practices; and societal protections and policies.

Each country received a score on each of the five criteria and these scores were combined into an overall index which could range from zero to 100. The index value for the United States was 70.4. It ranked 27th of the 82 countries i.e., it presumably (inferentially) provided its citizens with more opportunities for socioeconomic mobility than 55 other countries and fewer opportunities than 26 other countries.

The five countries with the highest 2020 WEF economic mobility scores were Denmark (85.2), Norway (83.6), Finland (83.6), Sweden (83.5). and Iceland (82.7). All of the countries in the top ten were European but the Nordic countries scored the highest. This is, no doubt, attributable to their (the Nordic countries) providing universal health care and free post-secondary education to their citizens as well as their having progressive employment practices and human rights statutes — all of which promote economic mobility. The data in the table on the next page show the previously-discussed 2020 Gini (income inequality) scores for the G7 countries along with their WEF economic mobility scores.

**2020 GINI COEFFICIENTS
AND WEF INDEXES: G7 NATIONS**

Country	Gini Coefficient (Income Inequality)	WEF Index (Economic Mobility)
United States	.434	70.4
United Kingdom	.392	74.4
Italy	.373	67.4
Japan	.363	75.1
Canada	.352	76.1
Germany	.351	78.8
France	.326	76.8

The 2020 Gini coefficients and WEF indexes for the G7 nations shown above are negatively correlated (- .61) which supports the contention that the higher a nation's economic mobility, as measured by the WEF Index, the lower its income inequality is likely to be.

Unfortunately, the level of income inequality in the United States (.434) is the highest of all the G7 nations while its economic mobility is the second lowest (70.4). This is not a desirable situation. High and growing levels of economic inequality and segregation combined with a relatively low level of social mobility can destroy social cohesion, foment dissatisfaction, and promote social unrest in any country.

The fact that America has a high level of income inequality

and a low level of economic mobility is ironic. Extreme income inequality combined with a low level of economic mobility was the major reason that Western Europeans came to America in the first place. Are contemporary Americans creating a class structure that looks more like the European class structures their forbearers sought to escape than the "American Dream" class structure their forbearers hoped to create?

The idea that economic equality, economic mobility and social cohesion go hand in hand is supported by the national happiness research data produced by the United Nations (U.N.). Each year the U.N. has a representative sample of the citizens in over 100 countries rate their happiness with the quality of their lives on a ten-point scale. Averages are then calculated for each country as a whole and for various subgroups in each country.

The 2019 U.N. World Happiness Report contained overall happiness scores for 156 countries. In 2019 the nationwide average score for the united States was 6.9, ranking it 19th highest of 156 nations. The top ten nations based on their 2019 average nationwide scores are shown in the table on the top of the next page.

2019 NATIONWIDE HAPPINESS SCORES

Country	Score (10-Point Scale)
Finland	7.8
Denmark	7.6
Norway	7.6
Iceland	7.5
Netherlands	7.5
Switzerland	7.5
Sweden	7.3
New Zeeland	7.3
Canada	7.3
Austria	7.2

Source: United Nations 2019 Happiness Report

The data in the above table show that the Nordic countries, those with the lowest economic inequality scores and the highest economic mobility scores, have the highest nationwide happiness scores. It is logical to infer from the happiness-score data that the Nordic countries are likely to have higher levels of social cohesion and lower levels of social unrest than other nations. The citizens of those countries are relatively happy with the quality of their lives and would probably agree that their countries are "on the right track."

CHAPTER 8:

SOCIOECONOMIC CLASS DETERMINATES

Socioeconomic class is about more than money. Meeting the income and wealth criteria described in Chapters 2 and 3 is necessary but insufficient for membership in the three-tiered upper class. There are a number of social criteria that also must be considered.

These (social) criteria fall into four groups — family background, personal achievements, appearance and behavior. How well Americans measure up on these criteria determines their **social status**. Their social status in combination with their income and wealth then determine which of the nine socioeconomic classes described in Chapter 3 they fall into. Thus, the proposed conceptual model is:

Economic Criteria = Income + Wealth

Social Status = Family Background + Personal Achievements + Appearance + Behavior

Socioeconomic Class = Economic Criteria + Social Status

Americans' social status has to do with how they are viewed by others i.e., their reputations. Those whose social statuses are high are respected, trusted and admired by others. People want to spend time with them, speak well of them, and want to see them succeed.

Social status is independent of economic status. One can be high while the other is low. Consider Elvis Presley. When he was alive his income and wealth were certainly higher than 99% of other Americans. Yet no one ever described Elvis as upper class. Next, consider Tiger Woods, the golfer. He certainly has the income and wealth to be in the upper-upper class but no one has ever described him as being so. There are many people who admire Tiger's golf game but not Tiger as a person. Thus, his social status and reputation keep him out of the upper class just as Elvis' did.

Now consider Reverend Martin Luther King Junior. His social status was extremely high. Millions of Americans respected, trusted, and admired him. He became a national hero while he was alive and a national holiday was created in his honor after he died. Yet neither his income or wealth were in the top 5% of Americans when he was alive and he was never considered a member of the upper class.

Then there was John F. Kennedy (JFK), the 35th president of the United States. If social status could be measured with precision his might be the highest ever seen in modern times. Millions of Americans respected, admired, and trusted him and millions voted for him to be President. The social status of George H. W. Bush, the 41st President, was probably a close second to that of JFK. Both JFK and Bush had Boston-Brahmin backgrounds and were considered to be "patricians." (Descendants of the ruling families of Rome as contrasted with the "Plebeians" or the common people of Rome.)

The social statuses of Mitt Romney and John Kerry are probably not far behind those of JFK and George H.W. Bush. All four of these men were or are members of the upper class because of their high social statuses as well as their income and wealth. The same cannot be said of Bill Clinton and his wife Hillary. Bill's income and wealth were not particularly high when he was elected the 42nd President of the United States and many Americans found his behavior while in office to be immoral and beneath the dignity of the presidency. (See discussion of a moral compass in Chapter 12.)

The social status of America's former President, Donald Trump, is certainly far below that of JFK. Despite living in New York, President Trump was never listed in the Social Register until he became president. After that, he was. The Social Register's policy has always been to list the President and Vice President of the United States.

Now ponder the question shown below. This question will be answered later in this book.

Which of the following contemporary Americans is likely to be considered a member of the upper-upper class? (Choose one response.)

> [a] **Jeff Bezos of Amazon**
> [b] **Bill Gates of Microsoft**
> [c] **Both of the above**
> [d] **Neither of the above**

CHAPTER 9:

FAMILY BACKGROUND

There are two aspects of an individual's family background that help determine his or her socioeconomic class. These are the socioeconomic class of the family he or she grew up in and the internal dynamics of that family.

Family Social Status and Socioeconomic Class

Coming from an upper-class family i.e., high social status **plus** high income/wealth is a plus and coming from a multi-generational upper-class family ("old money") is better yet. People who do so are typically given the benefit of the doubt by others; they inherit a presumption of superiority.

Then there is the matter of financial inheritance. Children raised in wealthy families benefit from that wealth while growing up and most of them also inherit meaningful financial assets. It will be recalled that, according to surveys by the Federal Reserve Bank, upper-income families (the top 5%) had median net assets of around $2,400,000 in 2016 (probably closer to $2,700,000 in 2020). Assuming that there are two children in each of these families, both children will inherit approximately $1,350,000. These amounts will no doubt be reduced by $300,000 or so by final expenses, attorney fees, and taxes leaving each child with a net inheritance of a million dollars or so.

Finally, there is the matter of connections. Upper-class families introduce their children to influential members of the community including the business community. These introductions and connections often turn out to be helpful to their children later in the children's lives and careers.

Internal Family Dynamics and ACEs

The internal dynamics of the families that children grow up in are at least as important as their families' social status and socioeconomic class. A relatively-recent, and often-referenced, study of the effects of early childhood experiences on adults was conducted in the late1990s by the U.S. Center for Disease Control (CDC) and Kiser Permanente, a large health maintenance organization in Southern California. Over 17,000 adult patients at Kiser Permanente completed questionnaires and in doing so described their early childhood experiences as well as their then-current health statuses and behavior.

This study was intended to investigate the effects, if any, of various adverse childhood experiences (ACEs) on adults. Three groups of ACEs were studied: abuse, neglect, and "household challenges." Each of these, in turn, was divided into subcategories. The five subcategories for "household challenges" were "Mother Treated Violently," "Substance Abuse in the Household," "Mental Illness in the Household," "Parental Separation or Divorce," and "Incarcerated Household Member."

The results of this study as well as similar studies that followed corroborated what mental health professionals already knew. Namely, that children exposed to large numbers of adverse childhood experiences are likely to have behavioral problems as adults. They are, for instance more likely to smoke, abuse drugs, and become more obese than their peers.

Dysfunctional Behaviors

In addition, some adults raised in high-ACE households exhibit high levels of insecurity and anxiety as well as low levels of self-esteem and self-confidence. As adults they avoid eye contact and generally seem more wary, and/or introverted than their peers. Many lack any semblance of a sense of humor and have difficulty establishing trusting and supportive relationships.

Other adults raised in high-ACE households exhibit behaviors generally associated with repressed anger. These behaviors include inappropriate emotional outbursts, as well as being overly-aggressive, cynical, and hostile in their dealings with others.

People exhibiting any of these behaviors are less likely to be trusted, respected and admired by others. Mental health professionals as well as sensitive and sophisticated laypersons notice dysfunctional behavior and when they do they are likely to question whether the individual exhibiting the behavior will be able to function well as an adult.

Post CDC-Kaiser research found that high-ACE households were typically headed by someone with a high-school education or less and that growing up in such households was, in turn, associated with poor academic performance and lower levels of academic achievement.

Deprivation and Discrimination

The CDC-Kaiser research as well as subsequent research inspired by it has not included **deprivation** (the regular or frequent lack of the basic necessities of life such as food, clothing, shelter, and health care) as a potential adverse childhood experience. In the writer's opinion however, deprivation, even without the presence of other ACEs, is sure to produce some of the same negative health and behavioral consequences as those associated with other ACEs. Growing up as a black or Hispanic American and being the victim of constant racial discrimination is, in the writer's opinion, also an ACE.

It is not **inevitable** that Americans who grow up in high-ACE households will have behavioral difficulties as adults. There may be persons inside or outside their households who provide them with the attention, love, and support they need to develop normally e.g., an uncle or aunt, a grandparent, a coach, and/or a boyfriend or girlfriend.

Internal Family Dynamics and PCEs

Children from married-couple, emotionally-stable, financially-secure families with parents that love them, support them, and set high expectations for them have presumably had many "Positive Childhood Experiences PCEs" (new term) e.g., parents helping them with their homework, going to parent-teacher conferences with them, taking them to concerts and sporting events, and listening patiently to their problems and concerns. PCEs are known to be associated with a number of positive consequences for adults such as enhanced self-confidence, emotional stability and the ability to establish stable and trusting relationships with others.

Tiger Moms and Helicopter Parents

"Tiger Moms" and "Helicopter Parents" — parents extensively involved in their children's development, are aware of the importance of positive internal family dynamics. They want their children to be happy and succeed academically. Such parents closely monitor their children's academic performance. In addition, they are concerned about their children's extracurricular activities. They take them to music lessons, ballet classes, soccer practices, summer camps, art exhibits and museums at rates and with intensities that amaze their friends. They take their children with them when they travel both domestically and overseas. They want their children to be well-traveled and they view such travel as "enrichment experiences".

One suspects that both Satya Nadella (CEO of Microsoft) and Sundar Pichai (CEO of Google), both of whom were born outside of the United States, came from families with excellent internal dynamics and perhaps Tiger Moms. If so, it may suggest that, in contemporary America, the internal dynamics of one's family are just as important as the social status and socioeconomic class of one's family in the determination of social status.

Tiger Moms and Helicopter Parents can, of course, go too far. They can, for instance, set unrealistic expectations for their children or demand so much from them that the stress they create causes their children to rebel or withdraw thereby creating "ACEs" and a toxic internal family dynamic. There is, however, little or no research showing this helicopter-parent burn-out syndrome occurring with any frequency.

Tastes and Values Acquired Through Osmosis

The French sociologist, Pierre Bourdieu, (1984) has pointed out that just by listening and observing their parents and other family members, children acquire class-specific tastes, and values through a process of osmosis — the unconscious assimilation of information through observation.

These osmosis-acquired tastes and values, in turn, influence how children choose to look (e.g., hair styles and make up), how they dress and how they behave even as adults. Children in upper-class families may, for instance, learn to place a high value on education, how to "dress for success," how to communicate with others in a restrained and respectful manner, how to entertain at home, and how to eat and drink properly simply by interacting with and observing other members of their families.

CHAPTER 10 :

PERSONAL ACHIEVEMENTS

People from upper-class families with positive internal family dynamics have a head start. They inherit a presumption of superiority. But that is not enough. How they do personally i.e., "on their own" particularly as teenagers and young adults is also important in determining their social status.

Personal achievements, academic and nonacademic, while in high school count. Did he or she graduate from high school? How well did he or she do academically? What about extracurricular activities? Any evidence of peer approbation or leadership?

A College Education

Getting into and graduating from college affects one's socioeconomic status in two ways.

First, it makes it more likely that one's income will eventually be high enough to meet the thresholds for entry into the middle-class and upper-class. There are major differences in earnings among people with different levels of educational attainment in America. These differences can be seen in the Census Bureau's annual household income data discussed previously as well as 2019 data produced by the U.S. Bureau of Labor Statistics (BLS) and shown in Chapter 4. (It will be recalled that the 2019 BLS data showed that the median annual earnings of individuals with Bachelor's degrees was $64,896 whereas the median annual incomes of individuals with only a high-school diploma was $38,792.)

The second way that getting into and graduating from college affects one's socioeconomic status has to do with personal prestige. According to the Census Bureau only one-third of today's working age Americans are college graduates. Not everyone can get into or graduate from college. Graduating from college is, therefore, considered to be an achievement. Many people look up to college graduates and are predisposed to defer to them, to think well of them.

Prestigious Colleges and Universities

There are a number of organizations that rank/rate American colleges and universities on a regular basis. Foremost among these is the U.S. News and World Report magazine (USNWR) which publishes its rankings annually. U.S. News uses a number of criteria in the determination of its rankings and these criteria have changed over the years. The two most heavily weighted now are the percent of students who graduate in six years or less after beginning their studies (only about 60% do) and "reputation data" (opinion survey data from college and university administrators). Other ranking/rating organizations use acceptance rates (the lower, the better) and/or average scores of in-coming freshmen on the SAT admissions test (the higher, the better). Regardless of the criteria used, the twelve colleges and universities listed in the table below are consistently ranked among the Country's most prestigious.

PRESTIGIOUS AMERICAN COLLEGES
AND UNIVERSITIES, 2020

Institution	USNWR Rank [a]	Acceptance Rate [b]	Freshman SAT [c]	Estimated Total Annual Cost [d]
Private, Ivy League				
Columbia	3	6.8%	1515	$79,161
Harvard	2	5.4	1520	73,799
Princeton	1	6.5	1500	73,027
Yale	5	6.3	1505	76,014
Private, Other				
Chicago	7	8.7	1530	78,900
MIT	4	7.9	1528	72,370
Northwestern	9	10.7	1490	76,889
Stanford	6	4.2	1465	74,450
Public				
California, Berkley	22	16.0	1430	66,756
Michigan	25	32.2	1415	72,200
UCLA	20	18.5	1405	66,521
Virginia	28	29.0	1365	74,362

Notes: [a] U. S. News and World Report, 2020 College Rankings [b] Percent of applicants admitted. Data shown from: The Education Corner, "College Acceptance Rates 2020," [c] average SAT composite admission test score, maximum score is 1600, [d] Includes undergraduate out-of-state tuition and fees, on-campus room and board, books, supplies and personal living expenses.

The Cost of A Four-Year College Degree

As the incomes of college graduates began to increase rapidly in the 1970s, the cost of a college education began to increase even faster. In the table below the 1970-2020 increase in the cost of tuition and fees (by far the biggest part of the total annual cost of going to college) at public and private U. S. universities is compared with the increases in median U. S. household income and the overall cost-of-living during the same fifty-year period. As the data in the table show, household income and overall the cost-of living increased approximately six-fold from 1970 to 2020 while the cost of tuition and fees at public and private collages increased twenty-six fold and twenty-one fold respectively — i.e., more than three times as fast as household income and the overall cost-of-living.

1970-2020 INCREASES

Tuition and Fees: U.S. Median Colleges and Universities				
Year	Household Income	CPI-U	Public	Private
1970	$9,870	37.8	$405	$1,792
2020 (est.)	63,500	258.0	10,500	38,000
2020/1970	6.4	6.8	25.9	21.2

Notes: [a] Income data are from Current Population Surveys, Bureau of the Census, [b] Cost of living, CPI-U ,data are from the BLS and, [c] tuition and fee data are from The National Center for Educational Statistics, U.S. Department of Education, 2019.

Growth In The Number Of Four-Year Institutions

The number of four-year colleges and universities has increased along with increases in the cost of a college education. According to the U. S. Department of Education there were 1,957 degree-granting four-year institutions during the 1980-1981 school year and there are approximately 2800 in 2020. Most of the increased supply of four-year institutions has come from the evolution of other types of postsecondary institutions. An example is shown in the box below.

1960: Valdosta Trade School

1970: Valdosta Vocational School

1980: South Georgia Technical School

1990: South Georgia Technical College

2000: South Georgia State College

2010: The University of South Georgia

Tuition and Fees v. Estimated Annual Costs
v. Actual Total Annual Costs

Tuition and fees is always the biggest of the four parts of the total annual cost of attending a college or university. The other three parts are room and board, books and supplies, and personal living expenses. Every year each college or university provides estimates of the total annual cost of attendance for various categories of students e.g., in-state, out-of-state, graduate, and undergraduate. Total annual cost estimates for the twelve prestigious colleges and universities named previously are shown in the table cited previously. The data in the table show that the institution-provided estimated average total annual cost for an out-of-state undergraduate living on campus at a prestigious American college or university now exceeds $70,000.

The total **actual** annual costs, what students actually pay however, are usually lower than the cost estimates provided by colleges and universities. There is plenty of competition among American colleges and universities for well-qualified students and this shows up in the increased availability of merit-based and need-based scholarships. These scholarships offer up to fifty percent reductions in tuition and fees and may cover other expenses as well. Thus, the total annual cost estimates provided by colleges and universities are similar to the "Manufacturer's Suggested Retail Prices" or "sticker prices" on new cars. They represent the upper limit of what students may be required to pay.

Based on the writer's review of a number of data sources it appears that the average **actual** annual total cost for an out-of-state undergraduate's attending a prestigious American college or university in 2019 was about $52,000 compared with the average university-provided estimate of over $70,000. The writer also estimates that the average **actual** annual total cost for an out-of-state undergraduate's attendance at a typical (not prestigious) American four-year college or university in 2019 was approximately $35,000.

2020-2022: A Buyers' Market

It is the writer's opinion that this figure ($35,000) is likely to **come down** in 2021. That is, that the actual cost of a college education in the United States will **come down** in 2020. One of the reasons for this is that the number of students in American colleges and universities has, for a variety of reasons, been declining — from about 20.5 million in 2011 to 19.0 million in 2019. This decline is likely to continue and the high cost of a college education is one of the reasons. Another reason that enrollments are likely to decline has to do with the current pandemic. It (the pandemic) will not only make it less likely that people will **want** to attend college in 2020-2021, it will also reduce the ability of middle-class families to pay for college.

This means that 2020-2022 will be a buyer's market for those seeking a college education in the United States — the first buyer's market in fifty years. The decline in enrollment in four-year American colleges and universities will cause a record number of them to go bankrupt and disappear. These will include a number of institutions established in the last thirty years. To offset the loss of income attributable to fewer American students attending college, the Nation's colleges and universities will probably recruit and admit record levels of foreign students nearly all of whom will pay full "sticker prices" for their educations

Student Loans

Even with the anticipated 2020-2021 reduction in the **actual** cost of college, a college education is still well beyond the means of lower-class and many middle-class families.

A number of years ago, the U. S. Federal Government decided to address this problem by guaranteeing the loans made to American college students by financial institutions i.e., "student loans." These loans were popular immediately and grew rapidly. The Federal Reserve Bank estimates that the total amount of student loan debt in the United States now exceeds $1.6 trillion and continues to climb. It is now higher than total credit card debt in this country and is exceeded only by total mortgage debt.

Lower-class and middle-class families welcomed the Federal Government's student loan program. They saw it as their children's bridge to college educations and middle-class lives. It turned out however, that government-backed student loans came with some unanticipated problems. Some economists, for instance, believe that the student-loan program itself was part of the reason for the dramatic acceleration in the cost of an American college education during the past fifty years. No matter how fast colleges and universities raised their fees, the federal government was there to provide money for students to borrow and pay back later. It was "free money" to some students and their families. Many of them borrowed as much as they could and today the average student loan debt for Americans graduating with a Bachelor's degree is about $30,000. This is a considerable amount of debt for a young person starting out.

The problem is worse for students who start college, borrow thousands of dollars and subsequently drop out. They may have accumulated $20,000 in debt and left with job and income prospects no brighter than when they graduated from high school. Even worse are instances where students started college, borrowed thousand of dollars, had their parents co-sign for loans, and then dropped out. Not only are those students in debt with no brighter job prospects than they had when they started; their parents are now also in debt or, as the case may be, more deeply in debt.

The Value Proposition

It may be that America's most prestigious colleges and universities provide their graduates with better educations than less-prestigious institutions do. But there is no clear evidence that this is the case. Americans do not need to complete comprehensive examinations in order to receive their Bachelor's degrees. If they did, it would be possible to answer such questions as "How much did 2020 mathematics graduates from Big Ten schools know vis-à-vis mathematics graduates from Ivy League schools?" and "Which college or university produces the most knowledgeable graduates in physics?". In the absence of comprehensive undergraduate examinations, questions such as these go unanswered. It is difficult, therefore, to prove that any one institution does a better job educating students than any another.

When making the decision to go to college or not and whether to apply to a prestigious college university or not, students and their families should remember that the greatest differences in earnings later in life are differences between college graduates and non-graduates, not between graduates from prestigious colleges and universities and graduates of less prestigious institutions. A well-qualified and highly-motivated student at a lesser-known college can learn as much or more than a graduate of a highly-prestigious institution. This is more true than ever in the age of the internet when students can supplement what they learn in class with what they learn on-line.

Having said this, the fact remains that graduates of prestigious colleges and universities are, and probably will continue to be, heavily recruited by employers. Recruiters know that not everyone can get into or graduate from a prestigious institution and that the graduates of such institutions were, at least when they applied for admission, among the Nation's best and brightest. These graduates often acquire or enhance a presumption of superiority.

"Class still counts"

This is not to say, however, that every graduate from a prestigious college or university will be heavily recruited by high-paying employers. That is simply not true. Nor is it true that a degree from a prestigious institution is a sure ticket to the upper class. How heavily a new graduate is recruited and how successfully he or she moves from college to a career is still influenced by his or her perceived socioeconomic class. Professor Lauren Rivera of Northwestern University conducted a multi-year study (See References) of the hiring practices of some of America's highest-paying investment banking, law, and consulting firms, what she refers to as "elite, professional service (EPS) firms."

The professor found that recruiters from EPS firms were most interested in graduates from highly-educated and high-income families (i.e., an upper-class family background), as well as graduates with significant personal achievements and those whose "appearance, language, and behavior" reflected an upper-class background.

Thus, even among graduates of prestigious colleges and universities, class still counts. Graduates from upper-class backgrounds have much better chances of being hired for high-paying jobs in EPS firms than do their classmates from middle-class and lower-class backgrounds. This is no doubt partially due to the fact that the members of EPS firms will be dealing with clients from upper-class backgrounds. It may also partially be due to the fact members of EPS firms want to work with people just like themselves — people with similar educations, backgrounds, interests, tastes, and values. To use the nine-story condominium analogy in Chapter 3, they want to work with and spend time with people " on the same floor."

"A college degree and a college education are not the same thing."

Finally, it should also be recognized that a college degree and a college education are not the same thing. Some people who go to college do so to party and/or acquire a credential, not to learn. They take the easiest courses possible, study as little as possible and graduate. The only time they were in a library was during freshman orientation. They have a college degree but not a college education.

Then there are people who went to college, worked hard, learned a great deal, and graduated. Since graduation, however, they have not read much other than the sports pages of their local newspapers and they rely on their cell phones to keep them up-to-date on world affairs. They have degrees but their college educations have expired.

Finally, some people have the equivalent of a college degree with respect to general educational development, critical-thinking skills, and occupationally-specific knowledge even though they never graduated from a college or university. They acquired knowledge and skills through experience, self-study and the internet. They have the equivalent of a college education without a college degree. There are plenty of them in the upper class and middle class. Perhaps Bill Gates of Microsoft is the most obvious example.

International Comparisons

The higher education system in America is excellent for those who can afford it but too many Americans cannot. It would be difficult to argue that America has gotten it right when it comes to higher education. Many other advanced countries including liberal democracies such as those in the U. K. and the countries in the European Union as well as autocratic "democracies" such as Egypt, Turkey, and Brazil provide their citizens with free college educations. It may only be a matter of time before some of those countries produce more scholars and scientists than the United States.

The high cost of a college education is a major reason for America's relatively low rate of inter-class mobility. It helps keep poor Americans out of the Country's four-year colleges and universities. It disadvantages poor Americans and helps keep them poor. It may be contributing to what appear to be rising levels of discontent and unrest among younger Americans

Occupational Prestige

In addition to their postsecondary educations, the type of work that Americans do also has a significant effect on their social status and socioeconomic class. The most comprehensive work on the prestige of various occupations in the United States has been done by the National Opinion Research Center (NORC) at the University of Chicago. In 1989 the NORC, based on extensive survey results assigned "Occupational Prestige Scores," which could vary between zero and 100, to over 800 occupations. Some of the scores are shown below. The NORC occupational groups are arguably overbroad. Neurosurgeon jobs at Johns Hopkins Hospital for instance, have much more status than family practitioner jobs in strip malls even though both are "physicians"

Nevertheless, it is clear that some occupations are far more prestigious than others It is also clear that the most prestigious occupations virtually all require a Bachelor's degree and are relatively high-paid when compared with other occupations. This is not always true, however.

Physicians (86.1)	Engineers (70.7)
Lawyers (74.7)	Accountants (65.4)
Architects (73.1)	Legislators (60.9)
College Professors (73.1)	Servers (28.1)
Judges (71.5)	Garbage Collectors (27.7)

There are prestigious and highly-paid jobs that do not require a college degree. For instance, entrepreneurs, entertainers, and professional athletes. There are also prestigious occupations that are not highly-paid. Consider the protective-service occupations.

Protective-Service Occupations

Ever since humans formed into groups, then tribes, then states for mutual protection, protective-service occupations such as police officers and fire-fighters have been respected and admired by others in the community. They serve and protect the common good. How many other occupations are there where people are continually thanked "for their service?" People holding these jobs are traditionally respected and admired by other Americans.

Perhaps the ultimate protective-service jobs in America are those in the Nation's military and intelligence services. In uniform or out these Americans defend and protect their countrymen on a daily basis and often at considerable risk to themselves. Members of the military are routinely thanked for their service and serving in the military is universally recognized in this and other countries as an honorable thing to do — something to be proud of.

There is a sharp dividing line in the military service, however, when it comes to occupational prestige and social status. Serving honorably in a non-officer role enhances an American's social status but serving as an officer enhances one's social status far more. Perhaps this is because ninety-nine percent of nonofficers are high-school graduates but only a handful are college graduates whereas over ninety percent of officers, are college graduates.

Performance-Based Occupational Prestige

No matter what one does for a living there is something to be said for being good at it. Being the best at what one does is even better — whether it is the best custodian, painter, programmer, minister, or physician. And it's not only a matter of personal pride although that's very important. It's also a matter of prestige and reputation. Americans respect and look up to people who are competent, perform well, and excel at what they do for a living.

When superior performance is recognized via awards, promotions or in other ways, one's prestige, reputation and social status are enhanced. Examples include graduating with honors, being elected president of a social or honorary fraternity, being promoted within a large organization and being elected an officer of a professional association.

Other Personal Achievements

There are still other personal achievements that can enhance one's social status These include community service activities such as serving on a town council or county commission, serving on the governing board of a religious organization, and excelling at a hobby of some sort e.g. playing in a local symphony orchestra, and being recognized for having the finest fly-rod collection in the Pacific Northwest. The list goes on.

CHAPTER 11 :
PHYSICAL APPEARANCE

The importance of appearance should not be underestimated. Looks matter. Americans are constantly observing one another's appearance and forming, confirming, or changing their socioeconomic class judgments based on those observations.

Physical Attractiveness

Americans are naturally drawn to physically attractive people. For whatever reason, they are interested in meeting them and spending time with them. There are social scientists who think that members of the upper class are generally (there are always exceptions) more physically attractive than other Americans, This assertion is probably impossible to prove or disprove. Those who think it is true argue [a] that the physically attractive tend to marry up in class whereas the less attractive marry down and [b] that members of the upper class have more time and money than other Americans to improve their appearance than with the help of orthodontists, plastic surgeons, and personal trainers.

Weight

According to the CDC, over one-third of American adults are obese and obesity rates are higher for lower-class Americans than they are for their upper-class counterparts. The comedian, Chris Rock, is quoted as saying that America is the only country where it's the poor people who are fat.

Quetelet's Body Mass Index (BMI) compares a person's height and weight and expresses the relationship in the form of an index. These indexes are summarized into weight categories such as those shown below.

> BMI <18.5   =   Underweight
> BMI 18.5 - 25.0   =   Normal
> BMI 25.0 - 30.0   =   Overweight
> BMI >30.0   =   Obese

There are a number of explanations for the higher levels of obesity found in the lower class. Perhaps the explanation on which there is the most agreement is that members of the upper class, because of their family backgrounds and higher educational levels, are more aware of the impact of diet on weight, health, and life-expectancy and therefore, make better decisions on what they eat and drink than do their lower-class countrymen.

Posture and Grooming

An individual's posture and grooming can affect his or her social status. Americans look positively on others with good posture, those who sit up and stand up straight. They also notice and admire people who are well-groomed — clean face, clean finger-nails, clean clothes and clean shoes. Poor posture and poor grooming inevitably have adverse effects on social status

Hair

Members of the upper class probably spend less time working on their hair than other Americans. Upper-class men, with few exceptions, decide on some sort of simple, conservative hair style early in life and never change it. They wouldn't think of changing their hair color, wearing a toupee, or sporting a comb-over. They are unlikely to have any form of facial hair such as a mustache or beard. If they do, the mustache or beard will not be extreme in any way and will be trimmed and groomed. As is true with hair styles, they make facial-hair decisions early in life and stick with them. Finally, the scruffy, need-a-shave look that seems to be gaining popularity among celebrities is a puzzlement to most upper-class men. To them, it is simply poor grooming.

Upper-class women are more likely than upper-class men to change their hair styles and color as they age, typically moving from longer to shorter hair and covering up the grey.

But they too tend to stick with simple, conservative hair styles and are not prone to experimentation. Lower-class American women, on the other hand. are more likely than any other socioeconomic class to change their hair style and color.

Teeth, Body Piercing and Tattoos

Other observable aspects of Americans' appearance that affect how others view them include teeth, body piercings and tattoos.

Teeth get noticed and can have a significant impact on how Americans see and react to one another. People with straight, white teeth have an advantage in that they are likely to be seen as more physically attractive than people with problem teeth. People with straight, white teeth often come from families that had the resources to get their teeth straightened when they were young. Others simply took care of it themselves in early adulthood. Cosmetic and orthodontic procedures are still relatively expensive in the United States so that straight white teeth are the norm in the upper class and problem teeth more common in the lower class.

According to research reported in the American Journal of Dermatology, soft ear-lobe piercing is common (>70%) among women of all socioeconomic classes. Other forms of body piercing e.g., nose, lip, and upper ear are relatively rare (20% of women and 8% of men). This second type of body-piercing declines with education level and income and is, therefore, far more common in the lower class than the upper class.

Approximately 20% of Americans have a tattoo of some sort most of which can be concealed with clothing. Younger people are more likely to have a tattoos than older people and the prevalence of tattoos declines with income and education. Tattoos, as is the case with nose, lip and upper-ear piercings, are far more common among lower-class than upper-class Americans. It is interesting to note that roughly 60% of people who have spent three or more days in jail have tattoos as compared with 20% of all Americans.

Make Up

The Merriam-Webster dictionary defines "make-up" as "… substances (such as lipstick and powder) used to make someone's face look more attractive." The use of make-up in one form or another goes back as far as ancient Egypt and has been controversial over years. In the 19th century, for instance, Queen Victoria declared that make-up was improper and vulgar.

In contemporary America "decorative" make-up products such as lipstick, blush, mascara, nail polish, and eye shadow are widely used by women. One explanation for this is that men are physically and sexually attracted to women who are healthy, attractive, and of child-bearing age i.e., relatively young. It's in the male DNA. Young, healthy, and attractive women have no trouble attracting men and they like it that way, want to keep it that way — it's in their (women's) DNA. Enter the decorative make-up products, nearly all of which are promoted as helping women look more attractive, healthy, and/or younger. Decorative make-up products are used by women at all socioeconomic levels but rarely by men. Skin-care make-up products such as cleansers and moisturizers, on the other hand, are used by men as well as women particularly in middle-class and upper-class families.

"Less is more"

It is the writer's experience that upper-class and upper-middle-class women are typically conservative and restrained with respect to the use of decorative make-up. To them, less is more and, with few exceptions, they use as little as possible.

Lipstick, (or lip gloss) is the most frequently used type of make-up and the overwhelming majority of women in all socioeconomic classes use it. The inter-class differences in the use of lipstick have to do with colors and enhancements. Some shade of red in a matte or satin shade is generally acceptable when used in moderation. Other colors such as blue and purple are used much less often and rarely by upper-class women.

The most common make-up decisions that harm the images and social status of contemporary American women have to do with excesses and substances that are additions rather than enhancements to the face. Excesses might include too much lipstick, blush (the second most-frequently used type of make-up) eye shadow and/or face powder.

Additions include false eyelashes, glitter, and paste-on beauty marks.

Finally, and as stated above, men at all socioeconomic levels might use skin-care products such as cleansers and moisturizers albeit not as frequently as women. The use of decorative make-up products by men of all socioeconomic classes is virtually unheard of.

Nails

Much of what has been said about make up applies to the maintenance and enhancement of fingernails and toenails. Less is more, excess is to be avoided, and the rules are different for women and men. Manicures and pedicures are very common among women, at all socioeconomic levels. Upper-class women typically have their nails done by manicurists or "nail technicians" but many women simply do them themselves. Most women also paint their own nails or have them painted. Some women glue-on fingernail extensions which make their fingernails look longer, sometimes much longer, than they actually are. It is the writer's experience that such extensions are much more common among lower-class than the upper-class women.

There is a nearly infinite variety of colors that women can be used to paint fingernails and toenails. Clear polishes or light shades of pink or red seem to be the choice of upper-class women. Lower-class women, on the other hand are much more adventurous when it comes to painting or otherwise decorating their nails. They may, for instance, paint some of their nails different colors than others or they may paint small pictures on one or more of their nails.

Manicures are relatively uncommon, although not unknown, among men at all socioeconomic levels and some may have their fingernails painted with a clear polish as a part of a manicure. The use of colored nail polishes by men is extremely rare.

CHAPTER 12:
CLOTHING AND ACCESSORIES

Clothing and socioeconomic class have been linked for centuries. In the late middle ages "Sumptuary Laws" in Europe regulated the clothing and accessories to be worn by members of various socioeconomic classes. A 1559 English proclamation, for instance, stated:

> "None shall wear in his apparel any cloth of gold, silver ...except earls, and all of superior degrees."

The nobles and aristocrats of those times wanted to be recognized as such and they sought that recognition through their clothing. Members of the middle class and lower class, however, chafed under the restrictions imposed by the Sumptuary Laws, particularly as new materials and types of clothing became available. These laws became increasingly difficult to enforce and over time they disappeared.

There were no Sumptuary Laws in the early American settlements and colonies. People could dress as they pleased. Neither was there much, if any, class-based differentiation in clothing among the farmers and shopkeepers of those times. As the economies expanded and the populations grew, however, social classes began to emerge. The members of the emerging American upper class i.e., the Boston

Brahmins, followed the example of the European aristocrats and sought to differentiate themselves from the lower classes in the colonies by the clothes they wore. They did so by wearing higher quality clothing and dressing more formally than other Americans. It could be said that they "dressed to differentiate" themselves and that they "dressed to impress" others.

A high-level of class differentiation in clothing persisted for the next 200 years in America, right into the 1950s. Pictures of crowds at 1950s sporting events like the World Series show upper class men in suits, dress shirts, and ties along with other men in the crowd dressed in casual slacks, short-sleeve shirts and no ties.

Inter-class differentiation in clothing may have peaked during the 1950s in America. If so it is ironic because that is probably the time that **intra-class** conformity also peaked. Members of the upper class and middle class sought to "fit in" by dressing like other members of the same socioeconomic class while also differentiating themselves from members of the lower class. This was the era of intra-class conformity, of the "organization man," and the "grey flannel suit." More Americans than ever worked in large organizations and what they wore was strongly influenced by what their superiors and co-workers wore.

"Sticking it to the man."

The cultural revolution that began in the 1960s and 1970s and that was referred to in Chapter 1 had profound effects on how Americans dressed. Prior norms and standards were challenged as never before in the Nation's history. As stated in Chapter 1, the overriding themes of the cultural revolution were a rebellion against social injustice and the desire for greater personal freedom.

The rebellion against pressures to conform and the desire for greater personal freedom started with teenagers and young adults. It was clearly evident when it came to clothing and music. In the big bands of the 1940s and 1950s the musicians wore matching suits or sport coats and played "easy listening" and "big band" music. In the "hard rock" and "grunge" bands of the 1960s, 1970s and 1980s, tee shirts, torn jeans, and leather jackets were closer to the norm and no two musicians looked alike. In addition, "hard rock" and its successor, "grunge" music, was anything but easy listening. It was the music of rebellion and resistance. As one famous rocker said "Rock and roll is all about sticking it to the man (i.e., authority)."

Changes in Fashion, Clothing, and Accessories

The rejection of pressures to conform as well as the desire for greater personal freedom spread into the middle class during the last half of the 20th century and brought about several changes in the world of fashion. First, there was greater acceptance of **diversity** in clothing and accessories. People had more freedom to express themselves in what they wore. Men and women dressed more colorfully than before. Many felt free to experiment with such innovations as "leisure suits," Nehru Jackets," mini-skirts, and the like.

The second change was that Americans began to **dress less formally**, more casually, than before. For male professionals and managers three-piece suits were seen less frequently and sport coats more frequently. "Casual Fridays" popped up in large organizations across the Country. Restaurants and private clubs revised their dress codes at a frantic pace. Many of them gave up dress codes entirely. Sales of men's neckties plummeted. Women professionals and managers replaced their suits and dresses with pants suits and sweaters.

A third change was from heavier to **lighter clothing.** Heavy corduroy, tweed and wool sport coats and suits gave way to new and lighter materials — even polyester, and spandex blends that would have been rejected by members of the upper class earlier in the century. One of the reasons for this was the new materials themselves. Garments made from these materials were lighter, softer, more wrinkle-resistant, and held up better than traditional all-wool garments.

Perhaps the movement from heavier to lighter clothing is also due to the fact that 21st-century Americans are warmer than earlier Americans. Climate scientists have shown that the average temperature in North America has been increasing for decades and that the pace of this phenomenon is accelerating. Another reason that today's Americans may be warmer is that the Country's population center has been moving from the northeast to the southwest states for more than 200 years. If a line were drawn from North to South through the United States in such a way that half of the population fell on either side of the line and a second line were drawn from east to west also bisecting the population, the intersection of the two lines would mark America's "population center." In 1800 the population center was near Baltimore. Today, it is about 600 miles southwest of Baltimore, somewhere in Missouri

And then there is the fact that the **relative cost of clothing** has come down sharply in the last half of the 20ᵗʰ century. The U.S. Bureau of Labor Statistics (BLS) reported that the overall cost of living for urban wage earners increased by 280% from 1980 to 2018 whereas the cost of apparel increased by only 20% during the same period. This made it much easier for Americans to have large and diverse wardrobes and to experiment with their clothing and accessories. The principal reasons for the lower relative cost of clothing are the same globalization and productivity-enhancing technology trends that are responsible for the loss of unskilled and semi-skilled jobs and the flat-lining of wages for blue-collar workers. It is far cheaper to manufacture garments overseas than it is in the United States. So much so, in fact, that it is hard to find clothing that is American-made.

The internet is another reason for the relative decline in the cost of apparel in this country. The internet makes it easy to compare the prices of alternative suppliers for the same or comparable items. Economists say that that the internet and companies like Amazon facilitate "price discovery" and comparison shopping thereby holding down prices.

Unwritten Rules

Despite the fact that contemporary Americans have much more freedom than their parents did when it comes to clothing and accessories, there are still unwritten social norms and standards i.e., rules with respect to what is acceptable. The extent to which people choose to acknowledge and conform with these rules still affects their social status — i.e., how others view them, whether they are respected and trusted, and whether others wish them well and want them to succeed.

Situationally Appropriate

The first of these rules is that one's clothing and accessories must be **situationally appropriate**. At work, apparel and accessories must be appropriate to the industry, the organization and one's role in the organization. Large hoop earrings, for instance, might be appropriate for a female account executive in a New York advertising agency or a set designer in a California movie studio but inappropriate for a female financial advisor in a New York bank. A camel-hair sport coat might be appropriate for a sales professional working for a manufacturing company in New England but inappropriate for the Marketing Vice President at the same company. It behooves new hires, therefore, to pay close attention to what people with whom they will be working wear to work and to use that information in making their own clothing and accessory decisions. To dress properly and appropriately at work demonstrates respect for one's employer and coworkers. Failure to do so demonstrates the opposite and has a negative impact on one's reputation and chances of being promoted.

Age and gender are also important considerations in choosing apparel and accessories. What is appropriate for a 25 year old administrative assistant may not be appropriate for a 50 year old administrative assistant and what is appropriate for a male accountant may not work for a female accountant.

It is important to recognize that dressing well at work does not mean dressing sexy. Women have more opportunity to do this than men but it is not likely to be helpful to their (women's) careers if they do. Cleavage, tight-fitting clothes, and short skirts will attract the attention of male co-workers but it's the wrong kind of attention. It is almost universally considered inappropriate by senior management and it raises questions about a women's character and taste. It will harm rather than help a women's social status and opportunities for promotion. It's generally considered to be a form of low-class behavior.

Proper Fit

A second unwritten rule at work and elsewhere is that clothing **must fit properly.** If it is too tight so that fabrics are being stretched, buttons are popping, and movement is restricted; others will notice and it will not reflect positively on the person wearing the clothing. Conversely, if clothing is too big others will notice and the social status of the person wearing the clothes will be diminished. The baggy, low-slung pants worn by some young men are a modern case-in-point. The young men who wear their pants this way may be doing so to enhance their reputation among their peers. For people outside of their peer group, however, the young men's baggy and low-slung pants seem disrespectful, inappropriate and in poor taste. This inevitably harms the young men's image, social status, and chances for advancement.

An example of the proper-fit mandate and how it has changed has to do with the length of men's pants. Today, men are wearing their pants shorter than men did just a decade or two ago. Now there is little, if any, shoe-top break in the pants, far less than there was at the turn of the century.

Good Condition

The condition of the clothing and accessories worn by Americans affects their social status and reputations. If their clothing is threadbare, faded, dirty, or torn their countrymen are less inclined to respect them or to admire them. If a physician has a broken watch crystal and food stains on her blouse, patients are less likely to trust her. It behooves people in jobs of all kinds to ensure that their clothing and accessories are in good condition. That includes being as clean, wrinkle-free and in good repair as possible.

A helpful habit in this regard is to rotate one's apparel and accessories. Wear a blue outfit on Monday and a brown one on Tuesday, a white shirt on Wednesday and a pink shirt on Thursday — never the same shirt or outfit two days in a row. Thanks to the decline in the relative cost of apparel this is something that virtually all Americans can do.

Coordination

Items of clothing and accessories should be coordinated. Three beautiful articles of clothing may look terrible when worn together — for example, a blue plaid suit, a red shirt, and a yellow tie or a golf outfit consisting of white shoes, ankle-length brown socks, red and yellow plaid shorts and a black shirt.

Patterns and fabrics should also be coordinated, not just colors. This is particularly true with respect to a man's jacket, shirt, tie, and pocket handkerchief. The coordination rule also applies to leathers i.e., belts, watch bands, shoes, handbags and brief cases. Blue and grey suits and jackets call for black belts, watch bands, shoes and brief cases.

Brown and tan suits and jackets call for brown leather. This may sound trivial but some job applicants have been turned down simply for wearing a white or tan belt and shoes with a dark blue suit to a job interview. Of course the applicant is never told that his or her clothing was the reason for the rejection. It's unfair but that's how it works. It works that way when being interviewed for memberships in prestigious clubs too. (Here it must be noted that the coordinated-leather rule is one of two unwritten rules of apparel that eluded George H. W. Bush during his presidency. The second is discussed later in this book.)

The level of formality of various items of clothing and accessories should also be coordinated. A broadcloth shirt with French cuffs is more formal or "dressy" than a shirt with a button-down collar and button cuffs just as a dark grey suit is more formal than a blazer and slacks. The dark grey suit should be worn with broadcloth shirts that have French cuffs and the blazer should be worn with button-down shirts.

The coordinated-formality rule extends to shoes. For men, lace-up leather shoes should be worn with suits whereas loafers and dressy slip-ons are fine with blazers and slacks. As this book is being written there is a regrettable fad with respect to men's shoes. It is the wearing of shoes that are not coordinated with suit pants or slacks. Instead, these shoes are designed to stand out, to make a statement. They might, for instance, be an uncoordinated color (e.g., tan shoes with a blue suit) and/or have the outer edges of the soles highlighted in white, yellow or some other stand-out color. These shoes make the wearers' feet look about twice as big as they are. Shoes such as these are in poor taste and destined to go the way of leisure suits.

Branded Clothing and Accessories

A variety of apparel items and accessories e.g., women's purses and athletic clothes in general, come with the manufacturer's name or logo clearly visible on them e.g., Nike basketball shoes, Gucci purses, and Lacoste polo shirts (alligator logo). These are very popular with young people.

Branded clothing and accessories can be appealing to the upper class but only if the apparel or accessory in question is of the highest quality and the name or logo is small enough to be discreet that is, you have to look for it. If it is so big that you can see it a mile away, it is considered to be gaudy and in poor taste. This same rule also applies to club-branded clothing and accessories e.g., country clubs, golf clubs and athletic clubs.

Learning the Rules

The situationally-appropriate, coordination, and branded-clothing rules can be confusing This is not surprising. The rules are, after all, unwritten. People from upper-class backgrounds sometimes, but not always, learn these rules by listening to their parents and peers and by observing what their peers and family members wear.

They and others can also find guidance on the internet, in newspapers and in magazines on what to wear and how to dress. And then there is observation. People can carefully observe what people of various socioeconomic classes wear and make their decisions accordingly.

Dressing For Success

In the middle and late 1970s, John T. Malloy investigated what successful members of the "upper-middle-class" (his term) wore to work. His findings were published in a series of books all of which included "Dress For Success" in the titles. Several of his books were best-sellers and contained valuable advice for people interested in improving their social status and moving up in the world. The advice he provided is consistent with the "Unwritten Rules" discussed above but more specific with respect to business attire for white-collar occupations.

For instance, his advice on the selection of men's suits stated:

> "The proper colors for a gentleman's suit are blue, grey, beige, brown and shades thereof. Any man who

sticks with those colors… will always be appropriately dressed."

He went on to state that solid color and (thin) pin-striped suits were always acceptable as were subtle (as opposed to loud) plaids. This advice with respect to the color and patterns of men's suits remains valid although it must be said that plaids can be troublesome in suits and sportscoats mainly because they are difficult to coordinate with shirts, ties, and pocket handkerchiefs. Solid color blazers are easier to work with in less formal situations.

Malloy's advice on shirts for middle-class and upper-class men also remains valid. He recommends sticking with white and solid colors (the paler, the better) and his forceful rejection of short-sleeve shirts for business wear is classic:

> "Short sleeve shirts are symbols of the lower middle class … upper-middle class executives…just do not wear short-sleeve shirts as well they shouldn't."

The no-short-sleeves rule was the second of the unwritten apparel rules that apparently eluded former President H. W. Bush. In his 2014 book, The Loudest Voice In The Room, Gabriel Sherman quotes Roger Ailes of Fox News and a consultant to Bush during the 1988 presidential election telling Bush "Don't *ever* wear that (short-sleeved) shirt again. You look like a f…ing clerk."

Yale University Research

Malloy's fundamental contentions that [a] one's dress affects how others perceive and interact with him or her and [b] dressing well improves one's likelihood of success in business were supported by research done at Yale University in 2014. In that research 128 men between the ages of 18 and 34 (probably students) were asked to negotiate with strangers (probably other students) for a valuable piece of property. Some of the negotiators were dressed in suits and some were dressed in sweatpants and plastic flip-flops. On average, the students dressed in suits did much better in the negotiations than those wearing sweatpants and flip flops. The prices they negotiated were almost twice as high as their less-well-dressed counterparts. Further, the researchers reported that the negotiators dressed in suits reported feeling significantly more confident and less willing to back down during the negotiations than their less-well-dressed counterparts.

Prices

As stated previously, the relative cost of clothing and apparel has been coming down in the United States but it can still be expensive. In the upper-upper class, it can be very expensive. At that level men's and women's suits and dresses are often custom made and cost upwards of $3,000 each. A custom-made tuxedo for an upper-upper class man (a must-have article of clothing at that level) can cost more. Tailors and dressmakers typically come to the homes and offices of the upper-upper class to fit and make this clothing. Suits and dresses in the lower two levels of the upper class are usually not custom made and cost $1,000 to $2,000 depending on the fabrics selected and the amount of tailoring required.

Shirts and blouses worn by members of the upper class are often, but not always, custom made and cost $200 to $400 each. Ties purchased by upper-class men typically cost between $50 and $100. There is, however, no need to pay upper-class apparel prices to look good.

One can, for instance, wait for sales. Plenty of the members of the upper class do. High priced clothing is often deeply discounted when it goes on sale. In addition there are bargains to be had at large department stores like Macy's and Nordstrom. If the unwritten rules discussed in this chapter are followed and conservative colors and patterns are chosen, a middle-class or lower-class man or woman can look like a million dollars in a $200 suit, a $25 shirt, and another $100 in accessories.

Accessories —
Hats, Ties, Pocket Handkerchiefs, and Jewelry

Hats, ties, pocket handkerchiefs , and jewelry are the most important accessory items for both men and women. They communicate a good deal of information about a wearer's taste and status.

Men's Hats

Men's hats have a long history in America. When the Country was being settled hats were broad-brimmed and functional. They protected settlers and farmers from the sun, the rain, and the cold. Western-style hats are still worn by many American farmers and ranchers. For a brief period, upper-class men wore stove-pipe top hats to signify their socioeconomic status. In the early 20th century, however, top hats gave way to fedoras, bowlers, and other dress hats for upper-class and middle-class men.

When John F. Kennedy was elected president in 1960, he did to hats what the automobile did to the horse and buggy. He almost never wore a hat and American men followed his example. Millinery (hat) shops, which were once as numerous as clothing stores began to disappear. In In 1978, the above-mentioned John Malloy wrote "… hats are optional" for middle-class and upper-class men and women. The movement away from dress hats was almost certainly helped along by the movment to more casual clothing and the warmer weather being experienced by so many Americans. Today dress hats are rare and of little social-status significance. The same cannot be said of baseball caps, however.

Baseball caps are seldom (there are always exceptions) worn to work by middle-class and upper-class men. Those same men, however, wear baseball caps for all kinds of outdoor activities including tennis, golf, gardening, attending sporting events, and running errands. Why? The principal reasons are that the caps help keep wearers warm in the winter, provide protection from the heat and sun in the summer, and keep the sun out of wearers' eyes year-round. They have lots of advantages.

Baseball caps are ubiquitous among people in the lower class, both men and women.

In the lower class, they are often worn to work as well as away from work. These caps typically have one-size-fits-all straps in the back and a company name, or a team name on the front e.g., "John Deere" or "New York Giants." For some reason, large segments of lower-class men wear their caps backward from time to time (thereby defeating the sun-protection benefit for which the caps were designed) and they wear their caps indoors. If caps are worn both backwards and indoors there can be no doubt about the wearer's socioeconomic class.

Men's Ties

As stated above, men wear ties less frequently than they used to do but ties are still required in some situations. When they are required they need to be color coordinated with shirts, pocket handkerchiefs and jackets. In almost all settings, ties should be silk or look like they are silk. Solid-color ties or ties with small dots are preferred. The bottom of ties should come down to the bottom of a man's belt buckle but not below it.

Pocket Handkerchiefs

Pocket handkerchiefs are more popular today than they were just a few decades ago, particulary for men. They can be worn in the jacket pockets of suit coats, sports coats, and blazers to add a touch of "class" (elegance.) They are worn more often in the middle-class and upper-class but they are also worn by fashion-consicious lower-class men. Pocket handkerchiefs should always be silk (like ties) and small enough to slip easily into jacket pockets, not bulky.

There are two basic options for the top of the pocket hand-kerchief: flat all the way across the top of the jacket pocket and multi-point. The former is more casual than the latter but both are acceptable. What is not acceptable are the cardboard squares with fabric stapled onto them that one sometimes gets from the cleaners.

Jewelry

The situationally-appropriate and coordination rules apply to jewelry. Consider watches, for instance. For discussion purposes watches can be divided into two categories: dress watches and sports watches. The dress watches worn by upper-class men are almost always thin gold or silver watches with leather bands. These watches are worn to work, and to social events. As suggested above, the leather bands should be coordinated with other leather items worn at the same time.

The sports watches worn by upper-class men are made to take a beating. They have heavy, reinforced metal or rubber cases and bands and they might have built-in stop-watch capabilities. Sports watches are worn for all types of outdoor activities and might also be worn indoors with sports coats and blazers. Solid gold sports watches, however, are universally regarded as ostentatious and gaudy and thus seldom worn by upper-class men.

Sports watches worn by women are much like the sports watches worn by men. The dress watches worn by upper-class women, however, are not the same as the dress watches worn by upper class men. Women's dress watches are thin and delicate and they typically have silver or gold, rather than leather, bands. They may also have diamonds or other precious stones in the bezels or faces of the watch.

It should be noted that the size (circumference) and complexity of watches has been increasing for a number of years. It has now reached the point where some of these watches are simply too big and too gaudy to be worn by ladies and gentleman. Some of them look more like something that Elton John would wear.

It is the writer's observation that upper-class and middle-class men seldom wear any jewelery other than a watch and possibly a wedding band. They are unlikely to wear other types of rings e.g., "pinky" rings, class rings, and/or bracelets.

In addition to a watch and a wedding ring upper-class and middle-class women may wear earrings, necklaces, bracelets and/or other rings. In a conservative work environment **or** in public they tend to stick with gold or pearl stud earrings and a thin necklace with or without a small pendant. In a less conservative work environment or a dinner out with friends they might wear diamond stud earrings, hoop earrings, a larger gold or pearl necklace and/or stacked bracelets.

Middle-class and upper-class women may bring out the bling for parties at private clubs, opening night at the opera, holiday parties and dressy dinners at friends' homes. The bling includes jeweled necklaces, bracelets, rings, and watches. Even in these instances, however, some restraint is exercised. Wearing a few pieces of quality jewelry is usually the choice of upper-class women. Wearing many pieces of costume jewelry is not.

Upper-class women are likely to coordinate their jewelry with what they are wearing e.g., a ruby ring with a red dress and an emerald ring with a green dress. Some women also coordinate metals whenever possible. If, for instance, a gold necklace is to be worn, gold bracelets, watches, earrings, and rings are chosen.

Finally, most middle-class and upper-class women are careful to consider whom they will be meeting with or dining with when deciding what jewelry to wear. If they are going to a holiday party with upper-class peers they might bring out the bling but if they are going to a family party with relatives from a variety of socioeconomic levels, they are very likely to show some restraint.

Prices for jewelry made with expensive components such as gold, silver, diamonds, and cultured pearls have not been coming down relative to other prices in the same way that apparel prices have. Today's technology, however, is such that faux jewelry such as manufactured diamonds is very difficult to tell from the real thing with the naked eye. This makes it possible for women at all socioeconomic levels bring out some bling when they wish to.

CHAPTER 13:

BEHAVIOR

The behavior of Americans plays a crucial role in the determination of their social status and socioeconomic class. Like appearance, behavior is observable and, therefore, different from other determinates of socioeconomic class such as family background and education You have no idea of someone's family background or education when you meet him or her for the first time. But, consciously or unconsciously, you do take note of someone's appearance and behavior when your first meet and, based on what you see and hear, you form an initial impression.

It does not stop there. Consciously or unconsciously, we take note of the behavior of people we already know and it either changes or confirms the impressions we have of them. Thus, behavior is inevitably one of the most important determinates of an American's social status, and socioeconomic class. In Europe as well as America, members of the upper class are expected to **behave as ladies and gentlemen** and to **promote the common good.** If they don't, their upper-class status will be in jeopardy.

The Common Good

In prehistoric times men and women formed groups and tribes for mutual protection and support. It was understood and later mandated that the members of a group or tribe support and protect one another and promote the common good. Behavior that harmed, endangered, or was offensive to other members of the group or tribe was discouraged or punished. Behavior that benefited or protected other members of the group, on the other hand, was looked on positively as were the people who exhibited such behavior. These people assumed leadership positions within their groups and tribes.

Warriors became chiefs, the most knowledgeable became teachers, and healers became medicine men and priests.

Later, groups and tribes became communities, states, and nations. But the common-good imperative never changed. The highest places in a community and a nation are reserved for those who are perceived as contributing the most to the common good. These are the people who are most trusted, respected and admired by other members of the community. People who clearly promote the common good at the expense of their personal interests are the most respected and admired of all. They are heroes.

History: Chivalry and Noblesse Oblige

The Code of Chivalry was developed in 12th century Europe. It mandated that noblemen (male members of the upper class) support the common good by obeying the laws of their nation states and mounting their horses ("Cheval" is the French word for horse) and defending their church and state whenever necessary. The Code also mandated that noblemen would never lie, always keep their promises, defend the weak (especially women), and be generous to all. This code was never reduced to a single, written document but it was well-understood by the knights and noblemen of the middle ages.

Many of these same concepts were inherent in the "Noblesse Oblige" philosophy which evolved in France several hundred years later. This philosophy held that aristocrats (men and women) were entitled to power, deference and respect but, in return, they had an obligation to be honorable and generous in their dealings with their lower-class countrymen.

Modern Expectations

Contemporary behavioral expectations for upper-class ladies and gentlemen have their roots in prehistoric times, the Code of Chivalry, and the philosophy of Noblesse Oblige but include additional, more modern, more nuanced expectations. Some of these additional expectations for gentlemen were described in a classic 1852 essay by Cardinal Newman, a prominent Irish Catholic educator. That essay is shown in Appendix A to this book.

In the essay, Newman begins by defining a gentleman as "… one who never inflicts pain" on others and, instead, seeks to help and support others (kindness). Further, Newman states that a gentleman is sensitive to the needs and concerns of others, open-minded, and reluctant to impose his own opinions on others. Newman also states that a gentleman "…has no ears for slander or gossip," "… is never mean or little (petty) in his disputes," and "…talks about himself only when compelled to do so."

Contemporary Unwritten Upper-Class Code of Conduct

Today's behavioral expectations for American ladies and gentlemen are summarized in the table below. These expectations can be thought of as an unwritten code of conduct for contemporary upper-class ladies and gentlemen. The genesis or origination of each of the expectations is also shown.

When George H. W. Bush died in 2018 the second most frequently-used word in his eulogies was "gentleman"; the first was "kind." Other frequently-used words in the eulogies included "gracious" (as opposed to petty), "restrained," "humble," "Patrician," "considerate," "courageous (physically and morally), and "role model." President Bush checked all of the boxes. He was a prototypical upper-class American gentleman.

Carriage, Deportment, and Social Skills

Ladies and gentlemen are expected to carry and deport themselves "properly" and in a dignified manner. They are expected to have good posture and to be unfailingly courteous and polite. Consistent with Newman's definition, ladies and gentlemen are expected to be restrained and reserved in their interactions with others. When they speak, they are expected do so in modulated tones, never loudly. They are also expected to avoid arguing with and interrupting others. They may gesture with their arms and hands but the gestures too are restrained. This is not to imply that members of the upper class are timid or weak. That is not usually the case. Instead, they are typically self-confident but not to the point of hubris or arrogance.

Upper-class ladies and gentlemen are typically comfortable meeting and dealing with people at all socioeconomic levels. They know how to make others comfortable often by asking them about themselves or discussing non-controversial subjects. They try to be positive and to avoid gossip, complaining, and whining. If they talk about money at all it is in terms of investments, never in terms of purchases or prices. As a consequence, other people like them, want to be around them, and say good things about them. Their social status is high.

It should be noted that the type of carriage and behavior described immediately above and expected of members of the upper class are not found only in the upper class. There are ladies and gentlemen in all socioeconomic classes. The carriage and behavior described above, however, are **required** for membership in the upper class. If an individual were to meet the income and wealth criteria as well as the other social status criteria described previously but fail to behave as a lady or gentleman, his or her reputation and social status would be severely damaged.

In addition to proper carriage and deportment, certain other social skills are expected of members of America's upper class. Among these are a more-than-basic understanding of food and wine, knowing how to dance, and knowing how to entertain in one's home.

UNWRITTEN BEHAVIORAL EXPECTATIONS OF CONTEMPORARY
UPPER-CLASS AMERICAN LADIES AND GENTLEMEN

Expectation	PH Genesis	CC Genesis	PNO Genesis	ME Genesis
Promote The Common Good	X			
Obey the laws of one's country	X			
Be loyal to, defend and serve one's country	X			
Be courageous morally and physically		X		
Be honest and keep promises		X	X	
Defend the weak, especially women		X		
Be honorable in dealings with others		X	X	
Be generous, charitable		X	X	
Be kind				X
Be sensitive, considerate				X
Be humble, restrained, not arrogant or boastful				X
Listen, be open-minded				X
Be polite and give no offense				X

Notes: PH= Prehistoric times, CC = Code of Chivalry, PNO = Philosophy of Noblesse Oblige, and ME = Modern Expectations)

"To live happily, live anonymously."

Upper-class Europeans have a saying: "To live happily, live anonymously." This is a philosophy that members of the American upper class, particularly the upper-upper class seem to fully endorse. With few exceptions, they try to "fly under the radar," stay out of the newspapers. Gated communities and unlisted telephone numbers are the norm. When they go out in public, they dress to fit in. Ostentation is avoided. No names on mail boxes, no bumper stickers and no window stickers that say "My daughter goes to WATTSAMATTA U." If they have any window stickers at all, they are parking stickers and those are as small as possible.

Eating and Drinking

How, what, and how much an individual eats and drinks is readily observable and will have an effect on his or her social status.

Table Manners

Especially important are table manners. Many job applicants as well as applicants for memberships in prestigious clubs have been interviewed at lunch or dinner and turned down because of their table manners. They are virtually never told that they were turned down because of their table manners which may seem unfair, but that's how it works. There are employers who will not hire people for sales or managerial jobs without having lunch or dinner with them. These employers may be seeking assurance that an applicant will be able to create the right impression and represent the organization properly or the employers may think that table manners provide some insight into an applicant's socioeconomic class and future behavior.

Table manners are not routinely taught in school. Since they are taught at home there are often differences in the table manners of people from different socioeconomic classes. A detailed discussion of table manners is beyond the scope of this book but some suggestions that may be particularly helpful to younger readers are shown below.

- Take the time to learn proper table manners as well as table settings i.e., where utensils and glassware go on the table. You will be more comfortable and self-confident when eating with your friends and family. This information is readily available and there is no reason for any American to have bad table manners.

- Don't slouch at the table. Ladies and gentlemen sit up straight with their napkins in their laps. Wait until everyone is served before starting to eat. If you are a guest, it is very important to wait until the host is served.

- **Eat like you are not hungry.** Ladies and gentlemen put their utensils down and engage in polite conversation between bites.

- Leave the salt and pepper shakers alone. Many chefs are offended when guests salt and pepper their creations.

- Do not wave your utensils in the air like a symphony conductor.

- Remember the **three bites rule** which applies in many dining circumstances. For instance if you are a dinner guest at someone's home and are served something you don't like, eat three bites of it and move on. Or if you simply must have some chocolate cake after a meal but you know you shouldn't, order the cake and eat three bites. The craving will disappear and you won't feel guilty.

There are two other table-manner issues that deserve mention. The first has to do with cell-phones. Non-emergency telephone conversations during meals with family members, friends, and business associates are rude and insulting to others at the table —simply bad manners and low-class behavior. This is also true with respect to extended personal conversations between any two people at a table in a larger group. People sharing a meal together have a responsibility to participate in conversations that involve as many people at the table as possible.

Food Choices

There are differences in the foods that Americans in different socioeconomic classes eat. Professor Adam Drewnowski of the University of Washington, a nationally recognized expert on this subject, points out that lower-class Americans tend to over-rely on "energy-rich" (high calorie), sweet-tasting, but nutrient-poor foods which can lead to obesity and related diseases such as diabetes. Researchers in the European Union have observed the same phenomenon in their populations.

The reasons given by researchers for the over-consumption of sweet-tasting, high-calorie foods by members of the lower class have to do with knowledge, cost, and accessibility.

That is, members of the upper class being generally better educated and knowing more about nutrition, diet, and health; are able to make healthier food choices. In addition, they have access to and can afford nutrient-rich foods such as fresh fish, fruits, and vegetables which are readily-available in their neighborhoods but may not be readily-available in poorer neighborhoods. It has been reported that 80% of the shoppers at Whole Foods (an expensive food-store chain that specializes in fresh and organic products) are upper-income college graduates.

Restaurants

Inter-class differences in food choices and preferences are readily observable in Americans' restaurant choices and behavior. According to a pre-Covid (2017) Gallup Poll survey about 35% of lower-class Americans go out to eat once or twice a week and when they do, they go to fast-food restaurants such as McDonald's and Kentucky Fried Chicken.

According to the same survey, fifty to sixty percent (50% to 60%) of middle-class and upper-class Americans go out to eat once or twice a week. Members of the middle class, however, tend to prefer "fast casual" as opposed to "fast food" places. Fast casual places include Mexican restaurants, pizzerias, and restaurants such Applebee's and Chili's. These places serve high-calorie food that tastes good and food that most Americans grew up with. Members of the lower-class and middle-class seldom try new foods. Surveys indicate that 30% to 40% of middle-class and lower-class Americans have never had sushi, prosciutto, escargot, gazpacho, or paella.

When upper-class Americans go out to dinner they might, on occasion, go to a fast food or fast casual restaurant but they are much more likely than their countrymen to go to up-scale, fine-dining restaurants. Members of the upper class are also less likely than their middle-class and lower-class counterparts to take advantage of 2-for-1, 20%-off or other types of restaurant incentives, Perhaps that is why it is rare for fine-dining restaurants to offer such incentives.

When members of the upper class in urban areas go out to eat it is likely that their first choice will not be a restaurant at all. Instead, they are likely to choose a private club of some sort, either a golf club, country club, or city club such as an athletic or university club.

Drinking

The results of a Gallup poll conducted in 2015 showed that about 64% of Americans drink alcohol. There were differences reported by education and income level. Eighty percent (80%) of college graduates reported that they drank whereas only 52% of those with a high school diploma or less said that they did.

Seventy-eight percent (78%)of people with annual incomes of $75,000 or more said that they drank while only 45% of those with incomes of less than $30,000 reported doing so. Since education and income are highly correlated with socioeconomic class, these data indicate that the percentage of people who drink increases as one moves up in socioeconomic class.

Beer (42%) is America's most popular alcoholic beverage followed by wine (34%) and liquor (21%). Among college graduates, however, wine (44%) is preferred over beer (35%) and liquor (18%). While the consumption of alcohol, especially wine is definitely a part of the life style of upper-class Americans, the over-consumption of alcohol is viewed as very offensive and irresponsible. Drinking too much is inevitably damaging to one's social status.

Moral Compass

American adults at all socioeconomic levels are expected to have a "moral compass," i.e., to know right from wrong and to always attempt to do the right thing. But how is one to know what is right and wrong? The answer to this question is that the right thing is always that which promotes the common good. One way to determine if a contemplated behavior promotes the common good is to ask, "What would happen if everyone were to do this or were to behave in this way? What kind of a family, an organization, or a country would this be?"

The Ten Commandments were some of the earliest mandates with respect to right and wrong. These emerged at a time in history when monotheism (the Judeo-Christian belief in one God) was replacing polytheism — the belief in multiple Gods that was held by the Greeks and Romans. The first few of the Ten Commandments mandate and endorse monotheism e.g., "Thou shalt have no other gods before me." But the others mandate behaviors that promote the common good e.g., "Thou shalt not kill," "Thou shalt not steal," and "Thou shalt not covet thy neighbor's wife" The Ten Commandments are clearly consistent with, if not driven by, the common-good imperative.

The common-good imperative is also the basis for laws established by states and nations. Behaviors that violate a nation's laws are also one of the surest and fastest ways to ruin one's reputation and lower one's socioeconomic class. This is why Americans who are convicted of violating the Nation's laws end up in the lower-class.

There are many behaviors that are immoral but not illegal. These too can be very damaging to one's social status. They include lying for purposes of self-aggrandizement, cheating, failing to keep promises, betraying confidences, and malicious gossip. Predatory and exploitive behaviors must also be added to this list. Some of these immoral, but not illegal, behaviors may seem trivial and unlikely to have any significant effect on one's reputation. This, however, is not the case. What may seem to be trivial transgressions such as betraying a confidence, misleading someone, or cheating at golf destroy trust, damage one's reputation, and do great harm to one's social status. This is particularly true in business where the credibility of one's "word" is critical.

And now to answer the question that was posed in Chapter 8: "Which American is more likely to be considered a member of the upper-upper class, Jeff Bezos of Amazon or Bill Gates of Microsoft?" The correct answer is 'Neither of the above.' Both Bezos and Gates are among the wealthiest people in the world but both were involved in extramarital affairs that ended their marriages, This cost them dearly with respect to their social status. Their divorces were not the problem; it was their dishonest and immoral behavior that led to their divorces.

The Power of "Thank You"

Upper-class Americans probably say "Thank You" more often and in more ways than any other Americans. Perhaps this is due to the fact that they have more to be thankful for. Perhaps it is something that they were taught early in life. Alternatively, perhaps they simply recognize the powerful positive effects that saying "Thank You" can bring. People at all socioeconomic levels appreciate being thanked and they are inclined to think more positively about, and want to do more for, those who thank them. It's human nature.

Simply saying "Thank You" is enough ninety-nine percent of the time. There are times, however, when more is required — a note or a small gift. Thank you notes are a specialty of the upper class. They often use personalized and engraved stationary for this purpose. Traditionally their thank-you notes are hand written in ink and mailed as soon as possible after a thankable (new word) event has occurred. In modern America a timely and thoughtful email will suffice.

"Timely and thoughtful"? Consider the following example: A

wealthy widow in Colorado took two of her teen-age nieces to the Brown Palace, a grand and historic hotel in Denver, for a holiday lunch. Three days later she received the following hand-written note from one of the girls:

"Dear Aunt Mary — thank you so much for Tuesday's wonderful holiday lunch at the Brown Palace. It was great to be with you and Polly again. I loved your red and green dress and I was glad to hear that you are doing so well. Mom and I are baking your favorite Christmas cookies and I'll bring some over next week. Looking forward to seeing you again.

Love, Terry Thoughtful"

Ten days later the widow received the following email from her other niece:

"Dear Aunt Mary — thank you so much for lunch. It was very nice. I meant to write you sooner but things have been crazy here lately." Merry Christmas.

Polly Perfunctory"

Which of the two nieces is more likely to become her aunt's "favorite niece?" Which of the two is Aunt Mary more likely to take to lunch again. Right! You get the point. It may not seem fair, but it's human nature.

Homes and Home Décor of The Upper-Class

According to the Census Bureau, approximately two-thirds of Americans live in owner-occupied homes. The other one third of Americans rent. The data currently available on second-home ownership in the United States are not particularly useful. Nevertheless it is a good bet that 20% or so of upper-class Americans and at least 50% of upper-upper class Americans own second homes. These homes may be close to their primary residences e.g., New York City - East Hampton, Denver - Snowmass, and Chicago - Door County; or they may be far apart e.g., Pittsburgh - Tampa; Salt Lake City - Scottsdale.

The primary residences of upper-class Americans exist in all kinds of communities across the Country. It is difficult to generalize, therefore, with respect to the style, size, and cost of these homes. It is fair to speculate, however, that upper-class Americans look for some of the same things that other Americans look for when purchasing a home e.g., solid construction, good condition, ease of maintenance, and location. In addition, however, upper-class buyers look for privacy, security, space, and distinctiveness.

Privacy is paramount. They would rather not see their neighbors and rather that their neighbors not see them. They prefer gated communities and large lots. They don't want to be close to public streets and roadways.

Security is also important whether their homes are in the city, the suburbs, or the country.

They are likely to make large investments in indoor and outdoor security devices, systems, and services. Space counts too. The homes of the upper class are likely to have a bedroom for every member of the household, a guest room or two, multiple sitting rooms and bathrooms, a large dining area, and a large kitchen. Additional rooms might include a home office, a library, a media room, a wine cellar, a billiard/game room and/or servants' quarters. The homes are likely to have high ceilings and an overall feeling of spaciousness. Upper-class buyers also look for distinctiveness — something unique, a "wow factor'" nothing "cookie cutter".

Members of the upper class and some members of the middle class expect to receive visitors and entertain in their homes. Members of the lower class typically do not. Thus, the interiors of most upper-class and upper-middle-class homes are usually maintained in "visitor-ready" condition. The home decors typically have a feeling of reserve and symmetry. The colors are muted and coordinated with occasional "pops of color." The ambiance is not unlike that in the lobby of a high-end boutique hotel.

The "public" areas of the homes, those used for receiving and entertaining guests, are uncluttered and depersonalized. Family pictures, trophies, religious articles, TV's, travel souvenirs, and pets are relegated to private (family) parts of the home.

The walls of upper-class homes are likely to be decorated with framed art — pictures of various kinds. The pictures may be paintings, photographs, posters, or something else. The art will typically be coordinated with other art in the same room e.g., all modern art in the same room or all western art. Various art objects a sculpture or a vase, may also be on display.

Language Skills

Upper-class ladies and gentlemen are expected to be well-spoken, not necessarily articulate, but well-spoken. They are more likely than their lower-class counterparts to speak in complete sentences, to pronounce words correctly, and to pronounce the "ings" at the ends of words they use. They also try to avoid annoying habits of speech such as [a] prefacing statements of their points of view with "Look" or "Let's be honest" [b] peppering their sentences with "like," and/or "sort of," and [c] over using "right?" as a rhetorical question.

An individual's language skills are, of course, heavily dependent on his or her vocabulary and knowledge of English grammar. While the available research on the vocabularies of contemporary Americans is inconclusive, there does seem to be some consensus on the facts shown below.

- Depending on how they are counted, there are 170,000 to 220,000 words in the English language lexicon.

- The average American adult uses about 20,000 words on a regular basis (active vocabulary) and recognizes another 20,000 or so upon hearing or reading them (passive vocabulary).

- One's vocabulary increases from birth to middle age — from zero at birth to 4,000 words at age 4, 10,000 at age 8, and 20,000 as an adult. After adulthood the size of one's vocabulary depends on what and how much he or she reads.

- Most television programming can be understood by someone with a vocabulary of 9,000 words —i.e., the vocabulary of an 8 or 9 year old (a 4th or 5th grader).

- The size of Americans' vocabulary increases with their educations and socioeconomic class.

Americans guess the socioeconomic class of other people all the time based on their vocabularies and grammar. Higher estimates might come about when "big" or unusual words are used and they might also come about when a variety of words (a large vocabulary) and/or "just the right" words are used. For instance, the adjectives "amazing" and "awesome" have seemingly driven all other adjectives out of the vocabularies of many middle-class and lower-class Americans. This is true even though those two adjectives are seldom "just the right" adjective. Would it not be better (more descriptive) to say that a flower is "beautiful" rather than "amazing"? Would it not be better to say that a close victory by a favorite sports team was "exciting" or "thrilling" rather than "awesome"? On the other hand, "awesome" may be just the right word to use when describing the Grand Canyon or the Rocky Mountains.

Relatively common vocabulary or word-choice errors today include "mute point" instead of "moot point"; "prostrate cancer" instead of "prostate cancer"; "exasperate" instead of "exacerbate"; and "irregardless" (not a word). A pet peeve of the highly educated is the use of the word "very" with unique — "very unique." Something is unique (one-of-a kind) or it isn't. The word "ain't" is in the dictionary as a contraction for am not, are not, and is not but "ain't" is a word that is rarely used by middle-class and upper-class ladies and gentle.

Double negatives ("I don't have no change.") are also assiduously avoided by members of the upper class.

Two other types of grammatical errors, mixed metaphors, and hyperbole also raise upper-class eyebrows and are damaging to one's credibility, reputation and social status. A metaphor is a comparison of two unlike things to make a point e.g., "She got here faster than a speeding bullet." The point is that she got here very quickly. Another popular metaphor is "More powerful than a locomotive." A mixed (nonsensical) metaphor would be "She got here faster than a speeding locomotive." Other mixed metaphor examples are:

- "Riding a dead horse."

- "Tom came out looking like a rose."

- "We'll burn that bridge when we come to it."

- "Fighting like fish in a barrel."

Hyperbole is excessive exaggeration and when it is for the purpose of self-aggrandizement it is extremely damaging to one's credibility and social status. An example is President Trump's description of the size of the crowds at his 2017 inauguration — "… far larger than the crowds for Obama's inaugurations" and "… by far the largest inaugural crowds in the Nation's history." Hyperbole such as this destroys trust and damages reputations.

Leisure Activities

Members of the Country's urban and suburban upper-class families have traditionally spent much of their leisure time at private clubs — both city clubs (e.g., university and athletic clubs) and country/golf clubs. According to the National Club Association there were more than 5,000 "full-service" private clubs in the Country during the 1990s and there are probably fewer than 4,000 today. Some of the reasons given for the decline in private-club membership include a decline in the number of Americans playing golf; the clubs' reputations for past discrimination on the basis of gender, race, and religion; younger people's preferences for more casual life-styles and fewer restrictions on their dress and behavior; and cost (typically $500 to $1,000 a month.)

Even with the decline in private-club memberships, upper-middle-class and upper-class families still spend a good deal of their leisure time at their clubs. There are many reasons for this — people are most comfortable around others in the same socioeconomic class, the club staff know them by name as well as their preferences and idiosyncrasies, and the food and service are usually superior. There is no doubt, however, that such clubs help perpetuate the economic segregation and reduced inter-class mobility discussed in Chapter 4.

Reading and Watching TV

According to the Bureau of Labor Statistics' (BLS) 2017 American Time Use Survey (ATUS), Americans age fifteen and over spend an average of approximately five hours a day engaged in some sort of leisure activity such as watching TV, socializing with friends or exercising. Watching TV accounts for over half (2.8 hours) of that time. The 2017 BLS ATUS survey also reported that Americans spend an average of twenty-eight **minutes** a day "reading for personal pleasure" and an average of nineteen minutes a day using the computer for pleasure (other than games).

The average American adult may spend about twenty-eight minutes a day reading for pleasure, but there are plenty who don't read books at all. A 2014 research report from the Pew Research Center stated that 23% of the American adults they surveyed had not read a book in the last twelve months and that another 28% had read one and only one. Pew also reported that reading books was positively correlated with education and income. If so, reading books is also positively correlated with socioeconomic class.

In summary, the available survey data indicate that Americans at all socioeconomic levels spend at least a couple of hours a day watching cable television or streaming- service programming e.g., Netflix, but that members of the upper class also spend a considerable amount of their leisure time reading books and magazines.

Sports

The Broken Clipboard is a website that focuses on the sociology of American sports. In a 2016 article published on the site, Taylor Hall discussed the sports preferences of various socioeconomic classes. One of his contentions is that members of the upper class (which he defines as the wealthiest four percent of the population) tend to prefer and pursue sports that are played at private clubs such as tennis, golf, squash, and swimming rather than sports that stress physical contact, violence, toughness and strength.

Further, it is Hall's contention that members of the middle class (which he defines as those with incomes of $50,000 to $150,000 a year) prefer team sports such as baseball, football, basketball, and soccer where there is some emphasis on toughness, speed and strength but also on traditional American values such as teamwork, sacrifice, and perseverance. Hall contends that members of the lower class (which he defines as those earning less than $50,000 a year) enjoy and participate in the team sports preferred by the middle class but also enjoy and participate in individual sports that involve violence, physical strength and danger such as weight lifting, boxing, wrestling, and automobile racing.

Sports on TV

The demographics of TV sports viewing audiences are interesting. In 2013 the National Hockey League (NHL) had the wealthiest audiences with 53% earning $75,000 or more a year compared with 43% for the PGA, and 33% for the NBA. NASCAR had the fewest viewers earning more than $75,000 — 28%

NASCAR had the highest percentage of white (94%) and women (37%) Americans in its viewing audience while the NBA had the lowest percentages of both white (40%) and women (37%) viewers.

Bad Habits

There are certain obviously dysfunctional and self-destructive behaviors that harm the images, reputations and social status of both men and women. Prominent among these are cigarette smoking, heavy drinking, problem gambling, and the use of illegal drugs. Each of these dysfunctional behaviors or "bad habits" is much more prevalent in the lower-class than in middle class and upper class.

The U.S. Centers for Disease Control and Prevention (CDC), for instance, has reported that cigarette smoking is twice as prevalent in the lower class as it is in the middle and upper classes. Further, research reported in the Lancet Journal of Public Health (2017) and elsewhere has consistently shown that alcohol abuse and alcohol-related diseases are found far more often in the lower classes in America and Europe than they are in the middle class and upper class. Other research has shown that lower-income/class Americans are more likely to become problem gamblers in casinos as well as the principal purchasers of tickets in state-sponsored lotteries.

This is not to say that no one in the middle class or upper class smokes cigarettes, buys a lottery ticket, goes to casinos, or smokes marijuana. That would not be true. It's just that these behaviors are much more prevalent among lower-class Americans. Thus, they are "clues" (see next chapter) that "Class Detectives" are sure to notice. The reader is urged to test the veracity of these assertions himself or herself by visiting a local gambling/gaming casino and observing the patrons. How many of them are smoking and drinking? What about their appearance and behavior? There will be a mixture of people from a variety of socioeconomic classes for sure but what percent appear to be from the lower-class, middle-class and upper-class?

Other behaviors that are harmful to the social status of Americans (but far less consequential then cigarette smoking, heavy drinking, problem gambling, and the use of illegal drugs) include chewing gum and using profanity. Chewing gum and using profanity are almost certainly more prevalent in the lower class than the middle class and upper class and the use of profanity is offensive to the majority of Americans at all socioeconomic levels.

CHAPTER 14:

THE CLASS DETECTIVE

Detectives in law enforcement agencies across America are good at reading people. Just by observing people's appearance and behavior and by listening to them speak, detectives can often make accurate guesstimates (new word) with respect to their socioeconomic class, their veracity, and their character (think moral compass). Good detectives can also "connect-the-dots," that is, make surprisingly accurate guesstimates with respect to the backgrounds and likely future behavior of people they come in contact with. This chapter asks you to be a "class detective" and complete three, two-page, three-part exercises.

Begin by reading the background information provided on the first page of each case and estimating the subject's income and wealth. These are never stated explicitly in the background information but a number of clues are provided. Next, estimate the subject's social status. This will require you to make some reasonable estimates with respect to the subject's family background, personal achievements (including education and occupation), appearance and behavior. Next, combine your estimates of the subject's income and wealth with your estimate of his or her social status in order to decide on your guesstimate of his or her socioeconomic class.

Part One

Indicate your guesstimate of the subject's socioeconomic class by drawing a circle around the name of one of the nine socioeconomic classes shown in Part One. If you can't decide between two classes, circle both of them.

Part Two

Next, complete Part Two on the first page of each exercise. Do so by putting a plus sign (+) in front of each of the clues that caused you to raise your estimate of the subject's socioeconomic class and a minus sign (-) in front of each of the clues that caused your to lower your estimate.

Part Three (Second Page)

Part Three of each exercise consists of a list of statements about each subject's past, present, and future. These are all inferences and predictions based on your estimate of his or her socioeconomic class which, in turn, is based on his or her appearance and behavior. Indicate how likely. in your judgment, each statement is to be true. Do so by placing a percent (e.g., 10%, 20% and etc.) in the space provided after each statement.

The writer's responses to Parts One, Two, and Three of each of the three exercises can be found in <u>Appendix B</u>.

CLASS DETECTIVE: THE FREQUENT FLYER MOTHER

Background

You have a mid-afternoon flight from St. Louis to Dallas. You are visiting your family for the holidays. You get to the American Airline's Frequent Flyer Club about one hour before boarding time. Shortly thereafter a mother whom you judge to be in her middle thirties arrives with her young son. He appears to be nine or ten years old. They take seats directly across from you.

She is an attractive white woman with dyed blond hair, beautiful teeth, very little make up, and a nice figure. Her son looks like her with blond hair and an athletic build. He is wearing black loafers, grey slacks, and what appears to be a school uniform blazer. The mother is wearing black wool slacks, black leather boots , a tan turtle-neck sweater and a camel-hair three-quarter-length   coat. The only jewelry she has on is a large diamond wedding ring and a Rolex sports watch. She reads an Atlantic Magazine while her son reads a book on his Kindle. They talk quietly until the boarding process begin

Socioeconomic Class Guesstimate (Part One)

What do you think the mother's socioeconomic class is? Answer by circling one of the nine choices shown below. If you can't decide between two choices, circle both of them.

Upper Lower	Upper Middle	Upper Upper
Middle Lower	Middle Middle	Middle Upper
Lower Lower	Lower Middle	Lower Upper

Clues (Part Two)

Place a plus sign (+) next to each of the clues listed below that raised your estimate of her socioeconomic class and a minus sign (-) next to each of the clues that lowered you estimate of her socioeconomic class.

1. Her being in the FF Club	6. Her jewelry
2. Her smile/teeth	7. The child's clothing
3. Her make up	8. The child's Kindle
4. Her physical attractiveness	9. The child's behavior
5. Her clothing	10. Atlantic Magazine

CLASS DETECTIVE: THE FREQUENT FLYER MOTHER (Part Three)

What is the probability that each of the following statements about the frequent flyer
mother is true? Answer in percentage terms (e.g., 10%, 20%, etc.) or write in "NI" for "No Idea".

IN THE PAST. She:

1. Was raised in a low-ACE household. ___%
2. Was raised in a high-income household. ___%
3. Experienced deprivation or discrimination while growing up ___%
4. Graduated from a private high school. ___%
5. Graduated from college. ___%
6. Once had a high level of student loan debt. ___%
7. Has been divorced. ___%
8. Has been the victim of violence, domestic or other. ___%
9. Once collected unemployment insurance. ___%
10. Used to be a pack-a-day cigarette smoker. ___%

AT THE PRESENT TIME. She:

11. Is married. ___%
12. Prefers bourbon over other alcoholic beverages. ___%
13. Has dinner parties in her home. ___%
14. Has a tattoo on the back of her right hand. ___%
15. Is a member of a country club. ___%
16. Is a member of a local book club. ___%
17. Is a NASCAR fan. ___%
18. Has an elaborate home security system. ___%
19. Is introverted and has a difficult time communicating with other adults. ___%
20. Lives in a gated community. ___%

IN THE FUTURE. She will:

21. Live several years longer than the average woman her age. ___%
22. Have several cosmetic surgery procedures before age sixty. ___% _
23. Leave it up to her son to decide if and where he will go to college. ___%
24. Be able to retire comfortably in her sixties. ___%
25. Become involved in various charitable endeavors. ___%
26. Ensure that her child is introduced to influential members of the community. ___%
27. Inherit a considerable amount of money. ___%
28. Have her hair cut short and dyed red. ___%
29. Be asked to serve on the Board of a local nonprofit organization. ___%

CLASS DETECTIVE: THE SERIOUS BOYFRIEND

Background

Your daughter is a senior at Columbia University in New York City. She called recently and asked that you and your wife meet her and her new "serious boyfriend" for dinner at a NYC restaurant. You and your wife arrive at the small Italian eatery before they do. You are wearing a blazer with an open-collar dress shirt and no tie. About half of the men in the restaurant are wearing jackets and the others are wearing sweaters. Jill and her new boyfriend, Jim, arrive shortly after you. Jim weighs about 235 pounds, and is 5'9" (two inches taller than Jill). He is wearing black tennis shoes, tan khakis, and a black sweatshirt with a Columbia logo. He has a small gold earring in his left ear. During dinner you learn that Jim was raised by his mother, a Nurse Practitioner in Buffalo, and that she and Jim's father, Physical Therapist, divorced when Jim was in the fifth grade. You also learn that Jim [a] is a senior majoring in photojournalism, [b] financed most of his college education with student loans and by working part time for a photographer in midtown, and [c] wants to work for a major metropolitan newspaper after he graduates. Jim is polite and well-spoken and his table manners are excellent. During dinner, however, he seems uncomfortable and avoids eye contact with you and your wife.

Socioeconomic Class Guesstimate (Part One)

Assuming that Jim and your daughter do get married and that he becomes a photojournalist for a major metropolitan newspaper, what socioeconomic class are they likely to fall into? Circle one of the nine below. If you can't decide between two choices, circle them both.

Upper Lower	Upper Middle	Upper Upper
Middle Lower	Middle Middle	Middle Middle
Lower Lower	Lower Middle	Lower Upper

Clues (Part Two)

Place a plus sign (+) next to each of the clues listed below that caused you to raise your guesstimate of Jim's future socioeconomic class and a minus sign (-) next to each of the clues that caused you to lower your guesstimate.

1. His being admitted to Columbia

2. His mother's occupation

3. His parents being divorced

4. His physical appearance

5. His clothing

6. His being well-spoken

7. His occupational plans

8. His table manners

9. Avoiding eye contact

CLASS DETECTIVE: THE SERIOUS BOYFRIEND (Part Three)

What is the probability that each of the following statements about Jim, the serious boyfriend, is true? Answer in percentage terms (e.g.,10%, 20% and etc.) or write in "NI" for "No Idea" in the space provided after each statement.

IN THE PAST, Jim:

1. Was raised in a low-ACE household. _____%
2. Was raised in a high-income household. _____%
3. Was raised by a "Tiger Mom." _____%
4 Was the victim of deprivation or discrimination while growing up. _____%
5. Got good grades in high school._____%
6. Has been the victim of violence, domestic or other. _____%
7. Has traveled out of the United States on vacation. _____%
8. Worked outside the home while in high school to support himself and his mother. _____%
9. Graduated from a private high school, _____%
10. Has a mother who is overweight _____%

AT THE PRESENT TIME, Jim:

11. Appears to be doing well in his studies at Columbia. _____%
12. Has a realistic and achievable career plan. _____%
13. Is outgoing and self-confident. _____%
14. Dresses well. _____%
15. Needs to improve his eating habits. _____%
16. Is a serious, hard-working young man. _____%
17. Uses illegal drugs on a regular basis. _____%
18. Smokes cigarettes. _____%
19. Drinks margaritas on a regular basis. _____%
20. Is an avid reader of travel and photography books. _____%

IN THE FUTURE, Jim will:

21. Live several years longer than the average man his age. _____%
22. Purchase a safe and comfortable home for himself and his family. _____%
23. Be able to retire comfortably in his sixties._____%
24. Have high-quality health-care insurance. _____%
25. Work a second job for additional income. _____%
26. Be able to send his children to college. _____%
27. Take his wife on a European vacation, _____%
28. Be a gentleman. _____%
29. Be a "Tiger Dad." _____%
30. See that his mother is well taken care of. _____%

CLASS DETECTIVE: THE ON-LINE DATE

Background

Your name is Kathy Williams. You are 28 years old and live in San Bernardino, California. You are single, never married, and the Head Teller at the Desert Bank and Trust. You met a man on line two weeks ago. The dating service informed you that Nick was 33 years old, single, lived in Ontario, California (about 20 miles from San Bernardino) and that he owned a dry cleaning business. You spoke to Nick on the phone and he seemed to be a nice guy so you agreed to meet him for dinner. When he picked you up he was driving a van and wearing jeans and a wrinkled golf shirt. He apologized for his appearance and said that he had come directly from work. Nick is a good-looking guy, about six feet tall, and in good shape. Nick drove the two of you to a country and western bar that he said had great food. During dinner Nick talked mostly about baseball and NASCAR and you noticed that he had a Dodgers logo tattooed on his right forearm. The bar was loud and the food was marginal although Nick seemed to like it. He had five beers and three cigarettes with dinner. (You don't smoke or drink alcohol.) He asked if you were willing to split the bill. You were and did.

Socioeconomic Class Guesstimate (Part One)

What do you think Nick's socioeconomic class is? Answer by circling one of the nine choices shown immediately below. If you can't decide between two choices, circle both of them.

Upper Lower	Upper Middle	Upper Upper
Middle Lower	Middle Middle	Middle Upper
Lower Lower	Lower Middle	Lower Upper

Clues (Part Two)

Place a plus sign (+) in front of   each of the clues listed below that caused you to raise your estimate of Nick's socioeconomic class and a minus sign (-) in front of each of the clues that caused you to lower your estimate of his socioeconomic class.

1. His van	6. His dinner conversation
2. His height and weight	7. His smoking
3.His clothing	8. His drinking
4. His tattoo	9. His occupation
5. His restaurant choice	10. Splitting the bill

CLASS DETECTIVE: THE ON LINE DATE (Part Three)

What is the probability that each of the following statements about Nick, the on line date, is true? Answer in percentage terms (e.g., 10%, 20%, and etc.) or write in "NI" for "No Idea."

IN THE PAST, Nick:

1. Was raised in a low-ACE household. ____%
2. Was raised in a high-income household. ____%
3. Was raised by a "Tiger Mom." ____%
4. Was the victim of deprivation or discrimination while growing up. ____%
5. Got good grades in high school. ____%
6. Graduated from college ____%
7. Served in the military ____%
8. Was divorced ____%
9. Was the victim of violence, domestic or other. ____%
10. Spent at least one night in jail. ____%

AT THE PRESENT TIME, Nick:

11. Rents a home or an apartment. ____%
12. Exercises regularly. ____%
13. Is a hard worker. ____%
14. Is an avid reader. ____%
15. Has season tickets for the L.A. Dodgers games. ____%
16. Loves to watch sports on television. ____%
17. Is going to college at night. ____%
18. Is paying child support. ____%
19. Is careful to dress well. ____%
20. Has health insurance. ____%

IN THE FUTURE, Nick will:

21. Live several years longer than the average man his age. ____%
22. Purchase a safe and comfortable home for himself and his family. ____%
23. Have high quality health insurance for himself and his family. ____%
24. Be able to send his children to college. ____%
25. Be unemployed. ____%
26. Graduate from college. ____%
27. Be recognized as a gentleman. ____%
28. Be a good husband. ____%
29. Own a vacation home. ____%
30. Be able to retire comfortably before he is 70. ____%

CHAPTER 15:
SUMMARY AND SUGGESTIONS

There were extreme wealth and life-style differences among people in different socioeconomic classes in 17th century Europe. The rich were very rich and the poor were very poor. There was little, if any, inter-class mobility. If you were born a peasant, your children were going to be peasants and you were going to die a peasant. The extreme inter-class differences in wealth and life-style as well as the lack of inter-class mobility were two of the principal reasons so many Europeans left their homes and migrated to the East Coast of the United States. They were in search of the American Dream — a more just and equal society where law-abiding and hard-working citizens could move up, could get ahead.

There was little in the way of wealth and life-style differentation among early American settlers. Such differences did, however, begin to emerge in the early 19th century in East Coast cities such as Boston and New York . The then-emergent group of wealthy land-owners, merchants and employers became America's first upper-class, the Country's first "elites." These people were referred to as "Brahmins," "Patricians," "Polite Society," and "WASPs (white, Anglo-Saxon. Protestants)."

Race, ethnicity, and religion played major roles (openly or not) in the determination of Americans' socioeconomic class from the early 19th century until World War II (WWII). During this period the Country was highly segregated by race and income. The members of the middle-class and the upper-class were almost entirely white and the members of the lower class were mostly black and Hispanic. Discrimination based on race and ethnicity were legal and white, black, and Hispanic Americans lived separate and different lives.

During WWII, however, Americans of all races, religions, ethnicities, and socioeconomic classes fought together shoulder-to-shoulder. They got to know each other as human beings. They realized how much they had in common and they earned each others' respect. Segregation based on race, religion, and ethnicity became less tolerable. The Country's armed forces were integrated shortly after WWII. In 1964 The Civil Rights Act was passed making it illegal to discriminate based on race, religion, or ethnicity in housing, employment and virtually all commercial transactions.

America's Golden Age

Right after WWII through 1975 the Nation's economy grew at an unprecedented rate. The Gross National Product (GNP) increased seven-fold. The world wanted what America was producing — refrigerators, automobiles, and airplanes and it wanted these things in quantity. American companies grew and their profit margins were high. American household incomes roughly doubled during this period and this was equally true for lower, middle, and upper-class Americans. Inter-class disparities in income growth had not yet emerged. Economists refer to 1945 through 1975 as "The Great Expansion" and "The Golden Age of Capitalism." It could also be called "The Golden Age of the Working Class."

The exhilarating and halcyon days of "The Great Expansion" came to an end in the last decades of the twentieth century. By that time America no longer had the world's markets for manufactured goods all to itself. Employers in other countries began producing refrigerators and automobiles and later airplanes and high-technology products. Profit margins for American manufacturers began to shrink and cost-cutting became imperative, not just to sustain profit margins but to survive in an increasingly-competitive world-wide economy. In order to reduce labor costs American manufacturers opened offices and plants in low-wage countries and contracted with suppliers in those countries. European and Asia manufactures also opened offices and plants outside of their home countries and the term "globalization" was born.

American manufacturers also attempted to reduce their labor costs by replacing blue-collar jobs with high-technology/automated equipment e.g., welding machines and computer-operated assembly equipment. These cost-reduction efforts on the part of manufacturing and even nonmanufacturing employers led to a reduction in demand for unskilled and semi-skilled blue-collar jobs in the United States. This, in turn reduced the bargaining power of unskilled and semi-skilled Americans as well as the unions representing them.

A Growing Income/Wealth Gap

Beginning in the 1970s the incomes of unskilled and semi-skilled blue-collar employees as well as lower-paid, white-collar clerical and technical employees began to grow more slowly than the incomes of upper-class professional and managerial employees. Perhaps more importantly, increases in the incomes of lower-paid blue-collar and white-collar employees failed to keep up with increases in the cost of inflation. Thus, many of these Americans could no longer afford the life styles they and their parents had grown accustomed to during the Country's Golden Age. This inter-class disparity in the growth of income and wealth has continued into the 2000s.

"Gini Coefficients" are commonly used to measure a nation's level of income inequality. These coefficients can range from zero (perfect equality) to 1.0 (perfect inequality). According to the Organization for Economic Cooperation and Development (OECD) the 2017 Gini Coefficients for the most economically developed countries (the G7 countries), ranged from a high of 0.434 for the United States to a low of 0.326 for France. Thus, income inequality in America as measured by Gini Coefficients is now higher than that found in any other large advanced economy. This inter-class disparity in income and wealth in America is now widely viewed as inequitable.

Economic Segregation and Inter-Class Mobility

As the incomes and wealth of upper income/class Americans began to grow faster than those of other Americans in the 1970s, the level of economic segregation in the Country also began to grow. The rich and the poor began living increasingly different lives. They no longer lived in the same neighborhoods. Their children went to different primary and secondary schools. A college education for their children as well as health insurance became increasingly unaffordable for lower income/class families. The rich and the poor no longer ate at the same restaurants or shopped in the same places. Today (2020) they don't watch the same things on television and the poor have only limited access to computers and the internet. Segregation based on race, religion, and ethnicity may be lower than it was prior to WWII but economic segregation is higher and economic segregation is just as painful to those who experience it.

A high level of inter-class mobility can take some of the pain out of economic segregation. A father might accept the facts that he and his wife will never go to college, own their own home, have decent health insurance, take a cruise, or retire if he thinks that his children will have a fair chance to live the American Dream. Unfortunately, the data show that the level of inter-class economic mobility in America is low relative to other economically-developed countries. Only about 4% of the children raised in the bottom quintile (20%) of the American income distribution make it to the top quintile as adults. This is reminiscent of 17th century Europe where if you were born poor, your children were going to be poor, and you were going to die poor.

A nation is asking for trouble when it combines increasing levels of income inequality and economic segregation with a low level of inter-class mobility. And yet, this appears to be what is happening in America in 2021. Data from the 2019 United Nations' <u>World</u> <u>Happiness</u> <u>Report</u> showed that the citizens of the United States expressed less satisfaction or happiness with their lives than did the citizens of eighteen other countries. Perhaps this should not be a surprise given America's rising levels of economic inequality and segregation and low level of inter-class mobility. Perhaps this explains why a large majority of Americans now think that the Country is "on the wrong track."

If unhappiness and dissatisfaction are the first levels on an "adverse societal consequences scale", what follows? Is it a breakdown in social cohesion accompanied by public demonstrations and protests? What about civil disobedience and rebellion?

A Proposed Nine-Level Class Structure

Two of the principal goals of this book were to provide a conceptual model of the Country's current socioeconomic class structure and to describe how the socioeconomic class of individual Americans is determined.

The proposed conceptual model of the Country's current socioeconomic class structure is presented and discussed in Chapter 3 and is shown below.

PROPOSED AMERICAN
SOCIOECONOMIC CLASS STRUCTURE: 2020

Class (% Of All Households)	Proposed 2020 Thresholds (Minimums)	
	Annual Income	Net Assets (Wealth)
Upper- Class (5%)	–	–
Upper- Upper	$400,000	$10,000,000
Middle- Upper	335,000	6,200,000
Lower-Upper	270,000	2,400,000
Middle-Class (70%)	–	–
Upper-Middle	< 270,000	< 2,400,000
Middle-Middle	160,000	250,000
Lower-Middle	50,000	1,000
Lower-Class (25%)	–	–
Upper-Lower	< 50,00	Zero
Middle- Lower	38,000	Negative
Lower-Lower	< 26,000	Negative

The Socioeconomic Class Determination Process

The **initial assignment** of each American to one of the nine classes in the proposed structure is determined by his or her household income and wealth. Income and wealth are the principal determinates of Americans' life styles. Their incomes and wealth determine the types of homes Americans live in, the cars they drive, the types of vacations they take, their health care, their children's educational opportunities, as well as if and how they retire.

While the **initial assignment** of Americans to one of the nine socioeconomic classes in the proposed structure is based on household income and wealth, the initial assignment may be modified, moved up or down, based on social status. One's social status has to do with how he or she is viewed by others, i.e., his or her reputation. Americans whose social statuses are high are respected, trusted, and admired by others. People want to spend time with them, speak well of them, and want to see them succeed. Social status is independent of income and wealth. One can be high while the other is low. Consider Elvis Presley. When he was alive his income and wealth were certainly higher than ninety-nine percent of other Americans. Yet no one ever considered Elvis to be upper class.

Four different sets of criteria are used to determine the social status of Americans: their family backgrounds, personal achievements, appearance and behavior. Thus, the proposed conceptual model for determining the socioeconomic class of Americans is:

Economic Criteria = Income + Wealth

Social Status = Family Background + Personal Achievements + Appearance + Behavior

Socioeconomic Class = Economic Criteria + Social Status

Coming from a high-socioeconomic-class family enhances one's own social status. Children raised in such families are seen as coming from "good families." They get a head start. But a head start is not enough. How they do personally, "on their own" is also important in determining their social status. An individual's education and occupation inevitably affect others' perceptions of him or her. Graduating from college is a plus, graduating from a prestigious college or university is a bigger plus.

The importance of appearance and behavior in the determination of social status should not be underestimated. Americans are constantly observing one another's appearance and behavior and forming, confirming, and/or changing their socioeconomic class judgments based on those observations.

Further, it is mandatory that members of the upper class behave as ladies and gentlemen. To fail to do so is to place one's upper-class status in jeopardy regardless of one's income or wealth. Members of the upper class know and understand the unwritten code of conduct for ladies and gentlemen in America. In addition, they have "moral compasses" and attempt to do the right thing — i.e., promote the common good. Immoral, but not necessarily illegal behavior such as lying for the purpose of self-aggrandizement, cheating, failing to keep promises, and malicious gossip are unacceptable. Predatory or exploitive behavior that adversely affects one's more vulnerable countrymen are equally unacceptable.

Troubling Signs

America's image around the world is slipping. During the Country's Golden Age (1945-1975) America was the most highly-regarded nation in the world. Millions of people from other countries wanted to come to the United States and live the American Dream. This, however, is not as true as it once was.

Every year Gallup conducts a survey among large, representative samples of people in more than 100 countries. Each survey participant is asked whether he or she has a favorable or unfavorable view of a variety of other countries and their leaderships. In **2016** America's "favorability rating" (The percent of survey participants with favorable views of America) was 48%. In pre-Covid **2019** it was down to 33%. By comparison, China's 2019 favorability rating was 32% and Germany's was 44%. These 2019 Gallup results are virtually identical to the results of a similar 2020 survey by the Pew Research Center. Both of these surveys found America's overall favorably rating to be in the low thirties and about the same as China's. The Gallup and Pew surveys were not conducted during America's Golden Age. If they were, it is the writer's opinion that America's favorability ratings then would have been in the high nineties

And then there is the annual Social Progress Index. Every year the Social Progress Imperative, a small think tank in Washington D.C. under the direction of Nobel-winning economists, analyzes fifty different measures of the quality of life in more than 150 countries. This survey focuses on objective nutrition, health, safety, and education measures (e.g., life expectancy, percent of households with internet access, and per capita suicides) and not the kind of subjective opinion data that the Gallup and Pew surveys so often do. In 2020 the Social Progress Imperative reported that, despite its wealth, (pre-Covid) America ranked 28th of 163 nations in overall quality of life. America ranked number one in quality of universities but number ninety-one in access to high quality primary and secondary education. It led the world in medical technology but was ninety-seventh in access to quality health care.

Domestically, a large majority of Americans now think that the Country is "on the wrong track," that it has lost its way. The June 2020 Harvard/Harris Poll, for instance found that only 27% of Americans thought that America was on the right track" while 64% thought that it was on the 'wrong track."

Suggestions

America, in the writer's opinion, is no longer the happy, highly-cohesive and optimistic nation it once was. Something has gone wrong. Its reputation among other countries is slipping. Its quality of life is no longer first among nations and its citizens are increasingly dissatisfied and restless. Why? What can be done to "right the ship," to make America a better place? The writer does not pretend to have the answers to such questions but does offer some suggestions immediately below.

Primary and Secondary Education

As has been shown previously, there is a strong relationship between income and education in America. A good place to start to address economic inequality, therefore, is to address the Nation's education system — its primary and secondary schools as well as its colleges and universities.

Every year the Organization for Economic Co-operation and Development (OECD) as a part of its Program for International Student Assessment (PISA) tests thousands of fifteen year-old students from countries around the world in math, science, and reading. It then issues a report comparing the students' test scores. In 2018, America's fifteen-year-olds came in 8th (of 79) in reading, 11th in science and 30th in math. Ominously, China's fifteen-year-olds came in first in each of the three categories. The OECD does not break out test scores by socioeconomic class. If it did there is no doubt in the writer's mind that American fifteen-year-olds from upper-class households would perform far better than those from middle-class and lower-class American households. It is also likely that the inter-class differences in America's test scores would be far greater than the inter-class test-score differences in other countries.

The American upper-class is giving up on public primary and secondary schools. When at all possible, they send their children to private schools. Even President Obama, a strong supporter of public education, sent both of his daughters to a private high school while he was President. According to a recent book by Daniel Markovits, (See References) over a quarter of children whose parents earn more than $200,000 a year now attend private secondary schools whereas as only about five percent of children whose parents earn less than $50,000 do. A reason that more parents do not send their children to private schools is simply the cost of doing so. Sending a child to a top private boarding school costs somewhere between $40,000 and $50,000 a year. Sending a child to a top private day school for his or her high school days costs between $25,000 and $40,000 a year. (The reader is reminded that these are not-for-profit organizations),

When they do send their children to public schools upper-class families supervise and supplement. That is, they become heavily involved in their children's educations — meeting with teachers, helping with homework, and planning curricula. They become "Tiger Moms and Helicopter Parents." They also supplement what the schools provide. They purchase computers and workbooks for their children, enroll them in commercially-available on-line courses, and take them to museums, art galleries, plays, and libraries on a regular basis. Public school systems in America have responded to this rejection by the upper class in a variety of positive ways. They have, for instance, established "magnet" schools and special interest schools such as fine arts" or "STEM" schools within their systems. On the other hand, a number of public schools have been forced to eliminate music and other "enrichment" programs due to a lack of resources.

Some of the most positive changes to the Country's public primary and secondary schools, in the writer's opinion, have come about as a result of President George W. Bush's "No Child Left Behind" initiative. Two mandates of this initiative are that learning objectives/expectations be established for individual classes and grade levels and that tests be used frequently to assess the extent to which the learning objectives have been achieved.

The specification of learning objectives keeps students and teachers focused on what is important and establishes a valid and objective **basis** for measuring performance. Testing to determine how well the learning objectives are achieved is also important. The test data can be used to evaluate and reward students, teachers and school administrators. The writer is aware that the "No Child Left Behind" initiative has been resisted by many primary and secondary school teachers and administrators. This should be expected. No one likes to have his or her performance expectations defined in highly-specific terms (learning objectives) and/or to have his or her performance closely monitored (frequent testing). Yet this is nothing more than good management and so is using student test data to evaluate and improve performance. Thus, the writer's first suggestions is that:

> 1. **America's primary and secondary schools should require the statement of learning objectives for all courses and grade levels, frequent testing to determine the extent to which those objectives are achieved, and the use of the test results to correct, reward, and improve the performance of students, teachers, and school administrators.**

It is recognized that this is little more than an endorsement of the "No Child Left Behind" initiative but if this suggestion is accepted nationwide it is likely to significantly reduce the inter-class education gaps in America that turn into income and social status gaps later in life.

The second suggestion for primary and secondary education is that:

> **2. Each student, beginning in the first or second grade and continuing through high school, should be provided with a laptop computer and internet access both at school and at home. Further, each student should be provided with regular instruction in the use of computers and the internet.**

Virtually all students from upper-class families have computers and internet access throughout their primary and secondary school educations. This gives them enormous learning advantages over students who do not have these things and perpetuates the digital divide between the rich and poor in America. The writer recognizes that providing laptops and internet access will involve addressing hundreds of financial and administrative issues in school systems but it is something that must happen soon lest the Country fall even farther behind other countries in terms of academic achievement of its young people.

The writer's third suggestion has to do with **HOW** students are taught in the Nation's primary and secondary schools i.e., teaching methodology. Many students are taught using the Lecture-Reading-Discussion-Application (LRDA) model (new term).

The LRDA model involves a teacher presenting/explaining a new theory or concept to a group of students (Lecture). This may be preceded and/or followed up by the students' reading related explanatory materials (Reading). The students then discuss the concepts or theories in class or attempt to apply the concepts by working on exercises or cases together (Discussion/Application). The weak link in this model is the Lecture. Teachers are human. They have good days and bad days. That applies to students also. They have good days and bad days. On good days everyone is focused and paying attention. On bad days teachers, students or both may not feel well, may be distracted or preoccupied and something is lost. Some days students are absent because they are ill or for some other reason. The writer's third suggestion with respect to primary and secondary schools is that:

> 3. **The initial presentation of new concepts and theories should be accomplished via recorded lectures presented in the classroom and/or available on-line to students 24/7 during the school year.**

The recorded lectures could be shown by teachers in classrooms and they (the lectures) would always be the teachers' best. Since the lectures would also be available on-line, students won't miss important information because they are were ill or because they or their teachers had a bad day.

Recorded lectures are likely to be particularly helpful to students from lower-income/class households. Many of these students come from troubled, dysfunctional (high ACE) households and have more trouble focusing and concentrating in class than their middle-class and upper-class counterparts. All students should be able to watch any on-line lecture over and over, as many times as they wish. Perhaps these lectures could be recorded at the beginning of each school year by classroom teachers or even by outside experts or celebrities. Classroom time could then be used to discuss and clarify theories and concepts as well as complete and discuss quizzes and exercises.

Even if students from lower-income/class households do as well academically in high school as their classmates from upper-class households they are likely to have a more difficult time getting into college or finding a good job after high school than are their upper-class schoolmates. Part of the reason for this is **connections** and **sponsorship.** Students from upper-class households are more likely to have parents and relatives who are influential and who know people who can help them get a job or into college. This is a tremendous competitive advantage.

Students from middle-class and upper-class backgrounds, because of what they learned through osmosis and what their parents and relatives taught them, are also more likely to have secured the sponsorship of adults outside of their families. Such sponsors might include former teachers, coaches, neighbors, and/or employers. Sponsors such as these are often won over not only by just a student's academic performance but also by the student's appearance and behavior — how he or she looks and dresses; his or her carriage, deportment, manners, language skills and integrity. Corporate recruiters and university admissions officers are won over by the same things.

Unfortunately, how to dress, look, and behave are not taught in primary and secondary schools. Those things are learned at home and from peers thus putting students from lower-class backgrounds at a disadvantage. It is the writer's opinion that such things should be taught in high school. It is suggested, therefore, that:

> **4.** **High-school students should have the opportunity to take classes focusing on how their appearance and behavior affects what others think of them (i.e. their social status).**

Perhaps such classes should be optional or perhaps there should be two classes, the first one mandatory and the second one optional. The course(s) would not be prescriptive — would not tell students what to wear or how to behave. The idea would be to make students aware of how their appearance and behavior affects what others think of them and then let the students choose how they wish to appear and behave. Such courses would probably work well on line. They might begin by presenting images of three different recent high-school graduates and asking students to write down their answers to a series of questions about each of the three subjects e.g., "Does this person look like someone you would like to spend time with, why or why not? or " Does this person look like someone you can trust?" and/or "Does this person look like someone you might want to be like?" After answering a few questions such as these the students could be shown answers to the same questions by other groups of people such as store managers, police officers, college recruiters, and/or bank loan officers.

The course(s) could also include brief videos of young people's behavior in different settings e.g., introducing one person to another, eating a meal, and/or providing a brief oral descriptions of their hobbies. This could be followed by asking the students a series of questions about the behavior they observed and then comparing their answers to the answers to the same questions by other groups of people.

Finally, the course or courses might involve field trips to observe how other Americans look and behave in different settings e.g., people applying for unemployment benefits, employees at a prominent law firm, prison inmates, and/or people entering a private downtown university or athletic club for lunch.

Students from low income/class households may need additional **personalized assistance** in order to perform well in public primary and secondary schools. Many public schools make this assistance available through Student Counselors, Student Advisors, or Student Advocates of one kind or another. Too often , however, the counselors or advisors in public schools have such large caseloads that they spend their time responding to crises rather than being proactive. For example, they may spend too much of their time with students who are about to be expelled for academic and/or disciplinary reasons and too little time sitting down with students at the beginning of each adademic year to decide on the courses the students should take and determining whether the students have the financial, emotional, and academic support they need to finish the academic year successfully. Thus, it is suggested that:

> 5. Primary and secondary students from low income/class households should be assigned to counselors/advocates who are proactively involved in helping them plan and successfully complete their academic studies as well as helping them secure the financial, emotional, and academic support (e.g., tutoring) they need.

The writer envisions these counselors meeting with their students once every two weeks or so and functioning more proactively and comprehensively than the typical overburdened public school counselor can. For instance, the counselors/advocates might develop comprehensive academic plans and schedules with students. Or they might help students with their nutritional needs e.g., arranging for free or subsidized meals at school as well as vouchers for meals on weekends if necessary. When necessary the counselors might put students in touch with outside organizations that can provide them with additional resources e.g., clothing, housing, and health care.

Proactive counselors/ advisors/advocates are readily available in private schools. There they take the place of, or work closely with, the Tiger Moms and Helicopter Parents often found in upper-class houselolds. The writer is aware that this recommendation would be expensive to implement. But what is the option? Students from lower-income/class households often come from troubled/dysfunctional households as well as households where the adults are both poor and poorly educated. Such students are simply not equipped to compete and succeed in competitive academic environments. They are programmed for failure and need help to succeed.

Tertiary Education Including Colleges and Universities

Most students from lower-income/class households need help even after they graduate from high school. Thus, four of the five suggestions stated immediately above also apply to colleges, universities as well as other tertiary education organizations. Specifically, such organizations should ensure that:

- All of their students are provided with laptop computers, 24/7 access to the internet, and related instruction as necessary.

- The initial presentation of new material is provided through recorded lectures that are available to students on-line, 24/7.

- Their students, especially those from low income/class backgrounds, are provided with the personalized, proactive, comprehensive counseling they need to succeed academically.

- Their students are aware of how their appearances and behavior affect how they are perceived by others and the consequences of those perceptions. (Classes such as those recommended above for high-school students could be designed and offered on a for-credit or not-for-credit basis for students attending colleges and universities. Such classes should be provided as soon as possible after students arrive on campus. Too often students from lower-class backgrounds never really "fit in" with other college students, become social isolates, ("dorm rats"), and leave without completing their degrees.

Two additional suggestions apply specifically to American colleges and universities.

Student Loans

As discussed in Chapter 10, the cost of a college education in America is now unaffordable for lower-class and many middle-class families. The Federal government has attempted to address this affordability problem with its guaranteed student-loan progam. It is possible, however, that years from now this program will be shown to have done more harm than good. It may have enabled, if not created, the hyper-inflation in the cost of an Amican college education. The universities knew that no matter how fast they raised their prices the federal government was there to provide the money for students to borrow and pay back later. And borrow they did. Total student loan debt now exceeds $1.6 trillion and it shows no sign of plateauing or declining. No other country has ever saddled its young people with so much debt at such a young age.

The federal government through its student loan program, grants, and scholarships probably accounts for more than half of the income of the Country's colleges and universities. The writer suggests that the federal government use its leverage to lower the cost of a college education for Americans. There are probably a number of ways to accomplish this. Here is one:

6. The federal government should revise its student-loan program based on each institution's tuition and fees for out-ot-state undergraduates relative to those of other institutions. Students attending schools in the 95%ile or above (i.e., the most expensive 5%) should be declared ineligible for such loans, students attending schools in the 90th through 94%ile should be are eligible for loans equal to no more than one-quarter of their tuition and fees, and students attending schools above the 50%ile should be eligible for loans equal to no more than one-half of their tuition and fees.

The formula suggested above may not be the right one and even if it is, it will need to be changed from time to time. But the reader gets the idea — the higher an institution's tuition and fees relative to a peer group, the less money available to it in the form of student loans from the federal government.

If this suggestion is accepted, the costs of a college education will come down. If the costs do not come down, the federal government should seriously consider declaring the highest-cost institutions ineligible not only for student loans but also for other grants and considerations including research grants. The federal government might ultimately consider revoking the tax-exempt status of those institutions whose high costs cannot be justified. The purpose of exempting an organization from federal taxes is to encourage and support organizations whose principal purpose is to contribute to the common good. It would be difficult to argue that a university which rejects over ninety percent of its American applicants, has a billion-dollar endowment, has a disproportionately large number of foreign students, and never lets a year go by without building at least two new buildings exists principally to promote the common good.

Accountability

And then there is the matter of **accountability**. To the writer's knowledge there is no proof that graduates from the Nation's colleges and universities know anything more when they graduate than they did when they began their studies. Learning objectives are rarely specified for individual courses and even more rarely for majors and degrees — e.g., "All students completing Sociology 101 will be able to explain the difference between ..... and ..." and "All students graduating with BS degrees in computer science will be able to .." How can colleges and universities demonstrate that they are indeed educating students — that their graduates learned something in college (i.e., longitudinal data)? Should some form of a comprehensive examination (something like the SAT) be required prior to graduation?

Further, is there any proof that the graduates with BS degrees in chemistry from MIT are better educated than graduates with BS degrees in chemistry from Cal Tech? Why isn't this type of cross-institutional comparative performance information available? It would be extremely helpful to high-school students and their parents in selecting a college or university. It might also prove useful when comparing America's colleges and universities with those in other countries e.g., China. Without such information how do American universities learn what and how they need to improve? This lack of accountability is simply poor management and it should not be tolerated by the federal government.

> 7. **The United States Department of Education, using its financial leverage, should require that all American colleges and universities develop and maintain relevant and objective data measuring their students' [a] intellectual growth (longitudinal data) and [b] comparing their students' intellectual growth and knowledge with that of students in other American colleges and universities (cross-institutional data).**

Ideally, the Department of Education will go farther. It might, for instance, develop data bases that allow it to compare the performance of American colleges and universities with colleges and universities in other countries. Perhaps it could adopt something like the OECD-PISA program and test representative samples of recent college graduates (instead of fifteen year olds) in OECD countries in reading, math, and science and compare the results.

Health Care, The Problem Is Cost

OECD studies as well as studies by the World Health Organization have shown that the world's finest and most advanced health care is available in the United States — if you can afford it. Members of America's upper class can afford it. They have their own concierge physicians and VIP suites in the Nation's hospitals and they live significantly longer than their middle-class and lower-class countrymen.

For the eighty million or so lower-income/class Americans, however, it's a different story. Approximately thirty million of them cannot afford health insurance. Many health-care economists belive that most of the other fifty million of the eighty million lower-income/class Americans are under-insured. Uninsured or under-insured, these people live in constant fear of losing everything they have due to an injury or illness in their family. This is not an unreasonable fear in America where the third leading cause of bankruptcy is the inability to pay health care bills.

It is well established that lower-income Americans put off seeking care for illnesses and injuries because of the costs of doing so. They also fail to fill prescriptions and/or take half-dosages of prescribed drugs for the same reason.

According to the OECD the 2019 health-care cost per capita in America was $11,072 and it was expected to increase to approximately $12,000 in 2020. The 2019 average health-care cost per capita in all OECD countries was $4,034. America's health-care costs as a proportion of its GDP have **nearly doubled since 1980;** from about nine percent to eighteen percent today. Health-care economists and politicians frequently speculate on why health-care costs are so high in America. What little consensus there is points to three major causes; prescription drugs, the overcompensation of physicians, and excessive administrative costs.

Prescription Drugs

The cost of prescription drugs accounts for about ten percent of America's total health-care costs and these (drug) costs have been increasing faster than overall inflation for a number of years. In 2019 and 2020 a number of studies reported that Americans pay as much as three to ten times as much for the same drug, in the same dosage as people in other countries. A large majority of these drugs are manufactured and distributed by American companies. Why is this? Why are Americans paying far more than people in other countries for drugs produced and distributed by American pharmaceutical companies and why are the costs of these drugs increasing so rapidly?

According to Wikipedia the answer to these two questions seems to be [a] federal government granted patents and monopolies to drug manufacturers as well as [b] other efforts by the federal government to support the Country's pharmaceutical firms e.g., prohibitions on importing drugs from other countries and prohibiting Medicare from negotiating drug prices with manufacturers. There are those who claim that the federal government has succumbed to the pressure of drug industry lobbyists to the detriment of the American people.

> **8. The federal government should do everything it can to stimulate world-wide competition for pharmaceutical drugs including the elimination of all restrictions and tariffs on imported drugs and permitting all federal agencies to negotiate drug prices. In addition, it should create and maintain a widely-available on-line database on the costs of all prescription drugs.**

It is noted that some commercial firms e.g., "Good RX", make on-line databases containing the cost of various drugs available to consumers free. If, for instance a consumer in Seattle wanted to know what different pharmacies in her neighborhood were charging for twenty 10mg tablets of Lipitor, she could go to the Good RX website and find out. Why doesn't the federal government make this information available? It is difficult to imagine that the Nation's pharmaceutical firms would oppose efforts to promote free competition in world-wide markets for their products.

Health Insurance

Approximately two hundred and forty million (240,000,000) Americans have some sort of health insurance. Most of them have employer-provided, private-sector health insurance. The others participate in government-sponsored health-care insurance programs (e.g., Medicare, Medicaid, the VA, and Obamacare.) It is a confusing, crazy-quilt of programs and it results in far higher per-capita health-care costs than the costs found in any other country. That, however, is not the biggest problem with health insurance in American. The biggest problem is that eighty million (80,000,000) Americans cannot afford insurance or that they are under-insured.

The cost of health-care insurance in the United States and the fact that so many citizens can no longer afford it have caused many to demand that the federal government take over the provision of health insurance for all Americans. This has become known as "Medicare For All." The basic idea is to enroll all Americans in Medicare, the federal government's popular health-care insurance program for Americans age sixty-five and over. "Medicare-For-All" is often referred to as a "single-payer program" because there would be only one insurer-payer — the federal government.

Some Americans are opposed to Medicare-For-All on philosophical and political grounds. They believe that it would entail the elimination of all private-sector health insurance and would be tantamount to "a government takeover of health-care" and "socialism." This, of course, would not necessarily be the case. A large majority of current Medicare participants purchase supplemental health insurance from private-sector insurance companies. It is should also be noted that survey after survey by the CDC and others show that eighty to ninety percent of Medicare participants are very satisfied with Medicare. It is the writer's view, however, that Medicare-For-All is not the answer to the Nation's current health-insurance problem The problem is that the cost of health care in America, including the cost of Medicare, is far too high. It doesn't matter who is paying the bills, the bills are too high — far higher in the United States than they are in other OECD countries.

The idea of a single-payer program is appealing nonetheless because it would dramatically improve the lives of millions of lower-income/class and middle-class families and help solve America's inequality problems. The idea of a single payer program is also appealing because it would probably bring down the Nation's overall health-care costs. In a recent (2020) study by the RAND Corporation (See References) it was discovered that hospitals were charging private-sector insurance companies more than twice as much as they were charging Medicare for the same services. Private-sector insurance companies simply do not have the negotiating leverage that the federal government does and they are forced to pay more thereby driving up theNation's overall health-care costs.

A single-payer program would also bring down the Nation's health care costs by dramatically reducing the administrative costs necessitated by administering so many different health insurance programs i.e., Medicare, Medicaid, Obamacare and the VA health care program. Therefore:

> **9.** It is suggested that and all-out effort begin immediately to drive down the cost of Medicare and that if these cost-reduction efforts are successful the federal government should rename Medicare to AmeriCare and expand AmeriCare to include all other government health insurance programs and to permit all Americans to enroll in AmeriCare on a voluntary basis.

How then to reduce Medicare costs? Here are four suggestions.

> **9a. Establish and maintain an on-line interactive Medicare Utilization Database.**

At the present time, a Medicare participant might decide to visit three different cardiologists and each of them might give the patient a different opinion and prescription, Further, it is entirely possible that none of the three physicians would know that the patient had seen another physician for the same problem. Medicare would likely pay for it all, including the prescriptions. This lack of information on the part of providers promotes over-utilization and unnecessarily high health-care costs. There should be an on-line database that providers could consult 24/7 to see a comprehensive and up-to-date record of each patient's medical history as well as his or her interactions with the health-care system in the preceding twelve months. Such a database would be extremely helpful in preventing over-utilization (abuse) as well as fraud. Later, the database could be expanded to include patient outcome data as well as cost-per-procedure information, This is the era of "big data" where computerized databases can contain a hundred million records, make each record instantly available anywhere in the Country and perform fast and sophisticated analyses of the information in a database. No one needs big data systems more than the federal government.

> **9b. Require all health-care providers who bill Medicare (including physicians, hospitals, and nursing homes) to publish the average prices they charge Medicare patients for services provided.**

These charges should be specified by procedure e.g., "knee replacement" or DRG. This information is simply not available currently and it would help bring down the cost of health care in America through improved "price discovery."

> **9c. Establish a means-tested co-pay policy for Medicare participants.**

One of the reasons that Medicare is so expensive is that it is over-utilized. It costs most seniors nothing out-of-pocket to visit their doctors and discuss real or imagined health problems with them.

And visit them they do. If there were a co-payment for each visit, something that seniors must pay out-of-pocket, it is likely that many seniors would think twice about scheduling unnecessary visits with their doctors and that the cost of Medicare as well as health care in general would come down. The co-payments could be determined by the participants' incomes as reported on their annual federal income tax statements. Medicare already has access to these statements and uses the income reported on the statements to determine the premiums that Medicare participants pay for coverage. The per-visit co-payments might be zero for participants earning less than $40,000 a year, $10 for those earning between $40,000 and $50,000 and so on.

9d. Subcontract Medicare fraud and abuse investigation to the private sector.

Every year claims managers in private-sector insurance companies read about physicians and medical laboratories who have defrauded Medicare and/or Medicaid out of millions of dollars and they ask themselves "How could this have happened?" Chances are that frauds of such magnitude would not happen to well-managed insurance companies Let private-sector health-care claims specialists handle Medicare claims processing and investigation, incentivize (new term) them properly and watch Medicare costs and health-care costs in general come down.

The Creation and Expansion of AmeriCare

Here's how it might work. Beginning on January 1st of the first year Medicare would be renamed AmeriCare and all Americans then enrolled in Medicare would be enrolled in AmeriCare. The cost-reduction efforts suggested above would begin. At the end of the first year if total AmeriCare costs are reduced by some predetermined amount (e.g., four percent) Medicaid would be eliminated and all Medicaid participants would be included in AmeriCare or all Americans sixty-three and older would be included in the program.

There are other options but the basic idea is expansion contingent on cost reduction.

At the beginning of the second or third year AmeriCare could be opened up to all Americans provided that they were willing to pay premiums sufficient to cover the cost of their participation in the program.

A Voluntary Health-Insurance Program

AmeriCare would be a completely voluntary health-insurance program for all Americans No one would be required to enroll in the program. There would still be a role for private-sector health-care insurance just as there is today. The creation and gradual expansion of AmeriCare would not be a government takeover of health-care insurance; would not be socialism. For many years the Nation's overall health-care costs would come down because of dramatically reduced administrative costs, an interactive patient-utilization database, means-tested co-payments, wide-spread availability of comparative cost data and more vigorous and sophisticated fraud and abuse prevention. More importantly, millions of Americans will lead better, more worry-free lives and American will be a better, more equitable Country.

Covid -19

When the final Covid-19 numbers are in they will undoubtedly show that lower-income/class Americans had higher infection, hospitalization, and mortality rates than their middle-class and upper-class countrymen as well as higher rates than the men and women in other all other OECD countries And it may get worse after the pandemic. Hundreds of Americans will lose their jobs and their private-sector health-insurance during the pandemic. Health-care insecurity may reach all-time highs in this Country.

Employee Benefits and Compensation

The United States is a nation of employees. Over ninety percent of Americans work for someone else — their employers. Employees need and appreciate income-protection programs. These programs protect their economic well-being as well as the economic well-being of their dependents when their employer-provided income is stopped or heavily burdened. The most important of these income-protection programs are health-insurance, life insurance, disability-income insurance, and retirement income programs.

These programs may be provided by employers, government agences or both. In the United States employee income protection programs are largely employer-provided. The federal government provides *de minimis* life insurance, disability income, and retirement income benefits through its Social Security program. For Americans age sixty-five and over the federal government provides comprehensive health-care benefits through Medicare. Turning sixty-five is a great joy and relief for many Americans.

American employers have a great deal of discretion with respect to the income protection programs and other employee benefits they provide. There is, for instance, no legal obligation for them to offer health-care insurance or any sort of retirement income program. This discretion has resulted in considerable employer-to-employer variation as well as considerable variation among groups of employees in the same organization with respect to employee benefits. An employer might, for instance, have a generous retirement income program for managers and executives and a less-generous retirement income program for non-managerial employees. This is also true with respect to paid leave. An employer might, for instance, provide salaried employees with fifteen days of paid vacation a year and hourly-paid employees with ten.

It is not difficult to understand why an employer would wish to differentiate among employee groups with respect to employee benefits. The problem is that it is inevitably lower-income/class Americans who are disadvantaged by the freedom to differentiate. It is they who worry most about about losing their jobs and their incomes when they are too old or too sick to work. This is not the case in other OECD countries where lower-paid employees are protected by strong "safety nets" of government-provided income protection programs. These other countries may be on to something. This may be another instance where the United States has gotten it wrong.

> **10. It is recommended that the Social Security be strengthened to provide sixty percent of pay for employees who cannot work for twenty days or more due to illness or injury and sixty-seven percent of final pay for employees who retire at age sixty-eight or more with at least 120 quarters of work.**

The formula specified in recommendation **10** above will need to be made much more detailed and specific and the details will need to be changed from time to time. The basic idea is that lower-income/paid employees should be provided with higher levels of income protection/security than is the case today and that the federal government should bare the principal responsibility for doing so. It should not be left up to the discretion of individual employers.

Inter-class income and wealth inequality and the resultant economic segregation increased sharply in the 1970s and continues to increase. This can be addressed by trying to limit the growth of the income and wealth of the upper class and/or by trying to accelerate the growth in the income and wealth of the lower-income/class. The writer prefers the latter option.

> **11. It is recommended that the minimum hourly wage in the United States be raised to $15.00 next January 1st and increased evey two years thereafter by a percentage equal to the percentage by which the average pay of of private-sector employees (as reported in the BLS Employment Cost Index) increased during the immediately-preceding twenty- four months.**

During the past three years many cities and several states raised their minimum wages to $15.00 an hour or more. When they did so, critics alleged that this was foolhardy and would cause many small businesses to fail and unemployment to rise in those areas. Now is the time to see if those were valid concerns/allegations. BLS or other researchers should compare employment and unemployment trends in cities and states with different minimum wage levels. The writer predicts that no evidence will be found proving that raising the minimum wage to $15.00 an hour will have resulted in more small-employer bankruptcies and/or higher levels of unemployment.

If an employee worked forty hours a week for fifty-two weeks he or she would work 2,080 hours a year. If the same employee earned $15.00 an hour, this would work out to $31,200 a year — a figure barely above the poverty threshold for a four-person household. An American earning working full time and earning this little would probably have little, if anything in the way of employer-provided benefits. Fifteen dollars an hour is not a "starvation wage" but it's not far from it.

CHAPTER 16:

CONCLUSION

The first few sentences in the first paragraph of this book are:

> "There probably has never been a society where everyone is treated equally. Inevitably, some people live better, are more respected, and have more wealth and power than others. There are different strata or classes in every society."

The United States in 2021 is no exception. Class is defined principally, but not entirely, by income in this Country. Upper-class Americans have far more wealth and power than middle-class and lower-class Americans. That's not the problem. The problem is that the income gap between upper-class and lower-class Americans has been growing for the last fifty years and has now reached the point where it is widely recognized as inequitable. Upper-class and lower-class Americans lead increasingly separate and different lives. America is no longer the happy, highly-cohesive, and optimistic place it once was. More and more members of the lower-class are leading "lives of quiet desperation."

A Changing Culture?

How did this happen? Some argue that the Nation's culture, its fundamental beliefs and values, has changed. Has America moved **from** a culture that once emphasized human rights, social justice, shared prosperity, and inter-class mobility **to** a highly-competitive, cutthroat, dog-eat-dog culture composed of winners and losers where there is little empathy, sympathy, or regard for lower-income/class Americans?

In the 2020 Democratic presidential primaries Tom Steyers and Elizabeth Warren expressed the view that American organizations of all kinds (for-profit and not-for-profit) prey on and exploit lower-class and middle-class Americans with the tacit approval of government officials. The number one exhibit has always been the American pharmaceutical industry where Americans pay two and three times what citizens of other countries pay for prescription drugs. These two politicians also point to the Nation's health-insurance industry as well as American colleges and universities both of which are world-class but unaffordable for many Americans.

Steyers and Warren could also have called attention to the fact that government-sanctioned predatory and exploitive behavior continues when members of the lower-class get home after work. When they try to relax and watch television with their families they are bludgeoned with far more (and often tasteless) commercials than would be permitted by the governments of other countries. Recall the "Evening News With Walter Cronkite?" That was an objective and sober reporting of the day's events with commercials accounting for twelve (20%) of sixty minutes. Some of today's (2021) evening news broadcasts are referred to as "Breaking News." or "Special Reports", titles intended to imply a false sense of urgency and/or importance. When did it become OK to mislead or trick other Americans? In addition, commercials now account for twenty minutes (33%) of sixty-minute news broadcasts. In addition, when a news anchor has to break for a commercial, he or she is more than likely to say "We'll be right back after a short break." and/or "Don't go anywhere." Who is misleading or tricking whom?

Will lower-income/class Americans continue to fall farther behind economically? Will their quality of life decline ever further? Or will the federal government intervene in some way to prevent this from happening? Has the Nation's commitment to free enterprise and competition resulted in unanticipated social and economic injustice? Is America evolving into an "everyone for himself" culture where predatory behavior and exploitative behavior are accepted? Do Americans now view one another other only as winners or losers. What happened to George H. W. Bush's call for a "kinder, "gentler" society?

Hopeful Signs

There are some hopeful signs — signs that some Americans see a need to improve the Nation's culture, to reduce economic inequality and segregation, improve inter-class mobility, improve the lives of Americans at all socioeconomic levels and protect lower-income/class Americans from being exploited and preyed upon by others.

Consider, for instance, "ESG" investing. The initials stand for (E)nvironmental, (S)ocial, and (G)overnance. The basic idea is socially responsible investing. ESG investors want assurance that the firms they invest in respect the environment (E). They also want assurance that the companies they invest in treat customers, employees,suppliers and the communities where they are located honestly and fairly (S).They want to know, for instance, how employees are selected, how much they are paid, and what sorts of income protection and paid-time-off programs are available to them. Finally, ESG investors are interested in a company's governance particularly its board of directors — how board members are selected and paid, how diverse the board is, and the transparency with which the board operates (G).

There are a number of mutual funds and exchange traded funds that now consist only of companies that meet ESG standards. These funds have sprung up in the last few years and have grown rapidly. Price, Waterhouse and Coopers recently (2020) completed a study that concluded, "ESG investing is the most significant development in money management since the creation of the exchange traded funds." ESG funds were not around in the 1960s and 1970s. In those days investors were urged to invest entirely on the basis of anticipated financial returns and to ignore ESG considerations.

A second hopeful sign is the Business Roundtables' (BRT's) recently-issued (2019) "Statement On The Purpose Of A Corporation." The Business Roundtable is a not-for-profit organization located in Washington D.C. Its membership is composed of the chief executive officers in large U. S. companies. Its stated purpose is to promote public policies favorable to business as well as broader public policies that promote the common good. For instance, it issued statements endorsing President Bush's "No Child Left Behind" initiative as well as statements opposing President Trump's family separation policies. The BRT is a highly prestigious organization. When it speaks, Washington and Wall Street listen.

In its 2019 "Statement On The Purpose of A Corporation" which was signed by nearly 200 chief executive officers including Jeff Bezos of Amazon, Tim Cook of Apple, and Mary Barra of General Motors, the BRT stated that it wished to move away from a "shareholder primacy" policy to a policy which places the interests of shareholders and owners on the same level as the interests of customers, employees, suppliers and communities. This recent BRT statement reflects a recognition on the part of the Nation's chief executives of the responsibilties they have to a variety of stakeholders including employees, not just shareholders. This is a hopeful sign to those concerned about income inequality and its corrosive effects in America.

Finally, there is the Pope. On October 3, 2020 Pope Francis, the head of the Roman Catholic Church, signed a papal encyclical. A papal encyclical is a letter from the Pope to Catholics around the world expressing the Pope's views with regard to the teachings of the Church. Encyclicals are written very infrequently and regarded as important by Catholic clergy and laypeople when they are written. The October 3rd encyclical was entitled "Fratelli Tutti" which can be literally translated as "Brothers All." The Pope, however, used the term to mean all men and women world-wide whom he sees as brothers and sisters in the same human family. In the encyclical the Pope endorses a "better kind of politics" i.e., one which rejects materialism, selfishness, and xenophobia, as well as one which fights poverty and inequality and strives to promote the common good. The term "common good" appears frequently throughout the encyclical.

ESG Investing, the BRT restatement of the purpose of a corporation, and Fratelli Tutti, could these be early signs of cultural changes to come in America and elsewhere? There will always be socioeconomic classes in a society but are these signs that America will be more focused on reducing economic inequality and improving the lives of lower-income/class Americans in the future? Time will tell.

REFERENCES: CLASS AND STATUS IN AMERICA

FREQUENTLY-USED DATA SOURCES

Criminal Justice, Ireasearch Net. Comprehensive criminal justice research and reference site. (http://criminal justice, ireasearchnet.com)

Gallup Incorporated, Washington D. C. public opinion surverys, (http://www.Galup.com)

Pew Research Center, Washington D. C, (http:pew research.org)

RAND Corporation, Santa Monica, California (http: RAND.org)

The American Psychological Association, (http://apa.org)

The Federal Reserve Bank, Washington D. C., "Survey of Consumer Finances".

United States Census Bureau, Washington D. C., (http:// census.gov)

United States Department of Education, Washington D. C., National Center for Educational Statistics, (http://nces.gov).

United States Department of Labor, Washington D. C., Bureau of Labor Statistics. (http://bls.gov).

OTHER WEBSITES CONSULTED

The Broken Clipboard. Website that focuses on the sociology of sports.

Quora. Open-access, question-and answer website with a strong emphais on class and status issues. (http://quora.com).

Wikipedia. Open-access, widely-referenced web-based encyclopedia.

JOURNAL ARTICLES

Chetty, Stepner, et. al., "The Association Between Income and Life Expectancy In The United States, 2001-2004", JAMA, 2016

Bishoff, Kendra and Sean F. Reardon, "Residential Segregation by Income", The Russell Sage Foundation, 2014.

John F. Sullivan

Fekitti, Anda et. al., "Relationship of Childhood Abuse and Household Dysfunction to Many of the Leading Causes of Death in Adults", American Journal of Preventative Medicine, vol 14, May, 1998.

BOOKS REFERENCED

A Social Critique of Judgment and Taste, Pierre Bourdieu, Harvard University Press. Cambridge. M.A., 1984.

Deaths of Despair and The Future of Capitalism, Anne Case and Angus Deaton. Princeton University Press, 2020.

Hillbilly Elegy, J. D. Vance, Harper Collins, New York, 2016.

New Dress for Success, John Molloy, Warner Books, New York. 1988.

Our Kids, The American Dream in Crisis, Robert D. Putnam, Simon and Schuster, New York, 2015.

Pedigree: How Elite Students Get Elite Jobs, Lauren A. Rivera, Princeton University Press, 2015.

The Loudest Voice in the Room, Gabriel Sherman, Random House, New York, 2014.

The Meritocracy Trap, David Markovits, Penguin Press, New York, 2019

The Velvet Rope Economy: How Inequality Became Big Business, Nelson D. Schwartz, Doubleday, New York, 2020.

The Years That Matter Most: How College Makes or Breaks Us, Paul Tough, Houghton, Mifflin, Harcourt, 2019.

APPENDIX A

"The Definition of a Gentleman"

by Cardinal Newman, from *The Idea of a University*, a series of lectures given in Ireland, 1852.

Hence it is that it is almost a definition of a gentleman to say that he is one who never inflicts pain. This description is both refined and, as far as it goes, accurate. He is mainly occupied in merely removing the obstacles which hinder the free and unembarrassed action of those about him; and he concurs with their movements rather than takes the initiative himself. His benefits may be considered as parallel to what are called comforts or conveniences in arrangements of a personal nature; like an easy chair or a good fire, which do their part in dispelling cold and fatigue, though nature provides both means of rest and animal heat without them. The true gentleman in like manner carefully avoids whatever may cause a jar or a jolt in the minds of those with whom he is cast --- all clashing of opinion, or collision of feeling, all restraint, or suspicion, or gloom, or resentment; his great concern being to make every one at his ease and at home. He has his eyes on all his company; he is tender towards the bashful, gentle towards the distant, and merciful towards the absurd; he can recollect to whom he is speaking; he guards against unseasonable allusions, or topics which may irritate; he is seldom prominent in conversation, and never wearisome. He makes light of favors while he does them, and seems to be receiving when he is conferring. He never speaks of himself except when compelled, never defends himself by a mere retort; he has no ears for slander or gossip, is scrupulous in imputing motives to those who interfere with him, and interprets everything for the best. He is never mean or little in his disputes, never takes unfair advantage, never mistakes personalities or sharp saying for arguments, or insinuates evil which he dare not say out. From a long-sighted prudence, he observes the maxim of the ancient sage, that we should ever conduct ourselves towards our enemy as if he were one day to be our friend. He has too much good sense to be affronted at insults, he is too well employed to remember injuries, and too indolent to bear malice. He is patient, forbearing, and resigned, on philosophical principles; he submits to pain, because it is inevitable, to bereavement, because it is irreparable, and to death, because it is his destiny.

If he engages in controversy of any kind, his disciplined intellect preserves him from the blundering discourtesy of better, perhaps, but less educated minds; who, like blunt weapons, tear and hack instead of cutting clean, who mistake the point in argument, waste their strength on trifles, misconceive their adversary, and leave the question more involved than they find it. He may be right or wrong in his opinion, but he is too clear-headed to be unjust; he is as simple as he is forcible, and as brief as he is decisive. Nowhere shall we find greater candor, consideration, indulgence: he throws himself into the minds of his opponents, he accounts for their mistakes. He knows the weakness of human reason as well as its strength, its province and its limits.

If he be an unbeliever, he will be too profound and large-minded to ridicule religion or to act against it; he is too wise to be a dogmatist or fanatic in his infidelity. He respects piety and devotion; he even supports institutions as venerable, beautiful, or useful, to which he does not assent; he honors the ministers of religion, and it contents him to decline its mysteries without assailing or denouncing them. He is a friend of religious toleration, and that, not only because his philosophy has taught him to look on all forms of faith with an impartial eye, but also from the gentleness and effeminacy of feeling, which is the attendant on civilization.

For further information, and to submit comments and suggestions:

APPENDIX B

CLASS DETECTIVE: THE FREQUENT FLYER MOTHER (Part One)

Background

You have a mid-afternoon flight from St. Louis to Dallas. You are visiting your family for the holidays. You get to the American Airline's Frequent Flyer Club about one hour before boarding time. Shortly thereafter a mother whom you judge to be in her middle thirties arrives with her young son. He appears to be nine or ten years old. They take seats directly across from you.

She is an attractive white woman with dyed blond hair, beautiful teeth, very little make up, and a nice figure. Her son looks like her with blond hair and an athletic build. He is wearing black loafers, grey slacks, and what appears to be a school uniform blazer. The mother is wearing black wool slacks, black leather boots , a tan turtle-neck sweater and a camel-hair three-quarter-length coat. The only jewelry she has on is a large diamond wedding ring and a Rolex sports watch. She reads an Atlantic Magazine while her son reads a book on his Kindle. They talk quietly until the boarding process begin

Socioeconomic Class Guesstimate

What do you think the mother's socioeconomic class is? Answer by circling one of the nine choices shown below. If you can't decide between two choices, circle both of them.

Upper Lower	Upper Middle	Upper Upper
Middle Lower	Middle Middle	Middle Upper
Lower Lower	Lower Middle	Lower Upper

Clues

Place a plus sign (+) next to each of the clues listed below that raised your estimate of her socioeconomic class and a minus sign (-) next to each of the clues that lowered you estimate of her socioeconomic class.

+ 1. Her being in the FF Club

+ 2. Her smile/teeth

+ 3. Her make up

+ 4. Her physical attractiveness

+ 5. Her clothing

+ 6. Her jewelry

+ 7. The child's clothing

+ 8. The child's Kindle

+ 9. The child's behavior

+ 10. Atlantic Magazine

- B1-

212

CLASS DETECTIVE: THE FREQUENT FLYER MOTHER (Part Two)

What is the probability that each of the following statements about the frequent flyer
mother is true? Answer in percentage terms (e.g., 10%, 20%, etc.) or write in "NI" for "No Idea".

IN THE PAST. She:

1. Was raised in a low-ACE household. 80 %
2. Was raised in a high-income household. 70 %
3. Experienced deprivation or discrimination while growing up 10 %
4. Graduated from a private high school. 50 %
5. Graduated from college 65 %
6. Once had a high level of student loan debt. 20 %
7. Has been divorced. 10 %
8. Has been the victim of violence, domestic or other. 10 %
9. Once collected unemployment insurance. 20 %
10. Used to be a pack-a-day cigarette smoker. 10 %

AT THE PRESENT TIME. She:

11. Is married. 80 %
12. Prefers bourbon over other alcoholic beverages. 5 %
13. Has dinner parties in her home. 80 %
14. Has a tattoo on the back of her right hand. 5 %
15. Is a member of a country club. 65 %
16. Is a member of a local book club. 70 %
17. Is a NASCAR fan. 10 %
18. Has an elaborate home security system. 70 %
19. Is introverted and has a difficult time communicating with other adults. 10 %
20. Lives in a gated community. 65 %

IN THE FUTURE. She will:

21. Live several years longer than the average woman her age. 80 %
22. Have several cosmetic surgery procedures before age sixty. 30 %
23. Leave it up to her son to decide if and where he will go to college. 20 %
24. Be able to retire comfortably in her sixties. 80 %
25. Become involved in various charitable endeavors. 50 %
26. Ensure that her child is introduced to influential members of the community. 80 %
27. Inherit a considerable amount of money. 50 %
28. Have her hair cut short and dyed red. 5 %
29. Be asked to serve on the Board of a local nonprofit organization. 40 %

- B2 -

CLASS DETECTIVE: THE SERIOUS BOYFRIEND (Part One)

Background

Your daughter is a senior at Columbia University in New York City. She called recently
and asked that you and your wife meet her and her new "serious boyfriend" for dinner at a
NYC restaurant. You and your wife arrive at the small Italian eatery before they do. You are
wearing a blazer with an open-collar dress shirt and no tie. About half of the men in the
restaurant are wearing jackets and the others are wearing sweaters. Jill and her new boyfriend,
Jim, arrive shortly after you. Jim weighs about 235 pounds, and is 5'9" (two inches taller
than Jill). He is wearing black tennis shoes, tan khakis, and a black sweatshirt with a
Columbia logo. He has a small gold earring in his left ear. During dinner you learn that Jim
was raised by his mother, a Nurse Practitioner in Buffalo, and that she and Jim's father,
Physical Therapist, divorced when Jim was in the fifth grade. You also learn that Jim [a]
is a senior majoring in photojournalism, [b] financed most of his college education with
student loans and by working part time for a photographer in midtown, and [c] wants to work
for a major metropolitan newspaper after he graduates. Jim is polite and well-spoken and his
table manners are excellent. During dinner, however, he seems uncomfortable and avoids eye
contact with you and your wife.

Socioeconomic Class Guesstimate

Assuming that Jim and your daughter do get married and that he becomes a photojournalist
for a major metropolitan newspaper, what socioeconomic class are they likely to fall into?
Circle one of the nine below. If you can't decide between two choices, circle them both.

Upper Lower	Upper Middle	Upper Upper
Middle Lower	Middle Middle	Middle Middle
Lower Lower	Lower Middle	Lower Upper

Clues

Place a plus sign (+) next to each of the clues listed below that caused you to raise your
guesstimate of Jim's future socioeconomic class and a minus sign (-) next to each of the clues
that caused you to lower your guesstimate.

+ 1. His being admitted to Columbia   + 6. His being well-spoken

    2. His mother's occupation   7. His occupational plans

− 3. His parents being divorced   + 8. His table manners

− 4. His physical appearance   − 9. Avoiding eye contact

− 5. His clothing   - B3-

214

CLASS DETECTIVE: THE SERIOUS BOYFRIEND (Part Two)

What is the probability that each of the following statements about Jim, the serious boyfriend, is true? Answer in percentage terms (e.g.,10%, 20% and etc.) or write in "NI" for "No Idea" in the space provided after each statement.

IN THE PAST, Jim:

1. Was raised in a low-ACE household. _50_ %
2. Was raised in a high-income household. _10_ %
3. Was raised by a "Tiger Mom." _50_ %
4 Was the victim of deprivation or discrimination while growing up. _50_ %
5. Got good grades in high school. _80_ %
6. Has been the victim of violence, domestic or other. _30_ %
7. Has traveled out of the United States on vacation. _10_ %
8. Worked outside the home while in high school to support himself and his mother. _15_ %
9. Graduated from a private high school, ____%
10. Has a mother who is overweight _70_ %

AT THE PRESENT TIME, Jim:

11. Appears to be doing well in his studies at Columbia. _80_ %
12. Has a realistic and achievable career plan. _90_ %
13. Is outgoing and self-confident. _20_ %
14. Dresses well. _10_ %
15. Needs to improve his eating habits. _80_%
16. Is a serious, hard-working young man. _90_ %
17. Uses illegal drugs on a regular basis. _10_ %
18. Smokes cigarettes. _5_ %
19. Drinks margaritas on a regular basis. _5_ %
20. Is an avid reader of travel and photography books. _70_ %

IN THE FUTURE, Jim will:

21. Live several years longer than the average man his age. _40_%
22. Purchase a safe and comfortable home for himself and his family. _65_%
23. Be able to retire comfortably in his sixties. _40_ %
24. Have high-quality health-care insurance. _75_ %
25. Work a second job for additional income. _50_ %
26. Be able to send his children to college. _65_ %
27. Take his wife on a European vacation, _50_ %
28. Be a gentleman. _80_ %
29. Be a "Tiger Dad." _65_%
30. See that his mother is well taken care of. _80_%

- B4 -

215

CLASS DETECTIVE: THE ON-LINE DATE (Part One)

Background

Your name is Kathy Williams. You are 28 years old and live in San Bernardino, California. You are single, never married, and the Head Teller at the Desert Bank and Trust. You met a man on line two weeks ago. The dating service informed you that Nick was 33 years old, single, lived in Ontario, California (about 20 miles from San Bernardino) and that he owned a dry cleaning business. You spoke to Nick on the phone and he seemed to be a nice guy so you agreed to meet him for dinner. When he picked you up he was driving a van and wearing jeans and a wrinkled golf shirt. He apologized for his appearance and said that he had come directly from work. Nick is a good-looking guy, about six feet tall, and in good shape. Nick drove the two of you to a country and western bar that he said had great food. During dinner Nick talked mostly about baseball and NASCAR and you noticed that he had a Dodgers logo tattooed on his right forearm. The bar was loud and the food was marginal although Nick seemed to like it. He had five beers and three cigarettes with dinner. (You don't smoke or drink alcohol.) He asked if you were willing to split the bill. You were and did.

Socioeconomic Class Guesstimate

What do you think Nick's socioeconomic class is? Answer by circling one of the nine choices shown immediately below. If you can't decide between two choices, circle both of them.

(Upper Lower)	Upper Middle	Upper Upper
Middle Lower	Middle Middle	Middle Upper
Lower Lower	(Lower Middle)	Lower Upper

Clues

Place a plus sign (+) in front of each of the clues listed below that caused you to raise your estimate of Nick's socioeconomic class and a minus sign (-) in front of each of the clues that caused you to lower your estimate of his socioeconomic class.

— 1. His van   — 6. His dinner conversation

+ 2. His height and weight   — 7. His smoking

— 3. His clothing   — 8. His drinking

— 4. His tattoo   9. His occupation

— 5. His restaurant choice   — 10. Splitting the bill

- B5-

216

CLASS DETECTIVE: THE ON LINE DATE (Part Two)

What is the probability that each of the following statements about Nick, the on line date, is true? Answer in percentage terms (e.g., 10%, 20%, and etc.) or write in "NI" for "No Idea."

IN THE PAST, Nick:

1. Was raised in a low-ACE household. 20 %
2. Was raised in a high-income household. 10 %
3. Was raised by a "Tiger Mom." 10 %
4. Was the victim of deprivation or discrimination while growing up. 70 %
5. Got good grades in high school. 45 %
6. Graduated from college 5 %
7. Served in the military 20 %
8. Was divorced 40 %
9. Was the victim of violence, domestic or other. 50 %
10. Spent at least one night in jail. 10 %

AT THE PRESENT TIME, Nick:

11. Rents a home or an apartment. 50 %
12. Exercises regularly. 20 %
13. Is a hard worker. 80 %
14. Is an avid reader. 10 %
15. Has season tickets for the L.A. Dodgers games. 10 %
16. Loves to watch sports on television. 70 %
17. Is going to college at night. 5 %
18. Is paying child support. 20 %
19. Is careful to dress well. 5 %
20. Has health insurance. 50 %

IN THE FUTURE, Nick will:

21. Live several years longer than the average man his age. 20 %
22. Purchase a safe and comfortable home for himself and his family. 50 %
23. Have high quality health insurance for himself and his family. 50 %
24. Be able to send his children to college. 40 %
25. Be unemployed. 10 %
26. Graduate from college. 0 %
27. Be recognized as a gentleman. 85 %
28. Be a good husband. 50 %
29. Own a vacation home. 10 %
30. Be able to retire comfortable before he is 70. 20 %

- B6-

217

CPSIA information can be obtained
at www.ICGtesting.com
Printed in the USA
LVHW052123131021
700374LV00004B/12/J